100 READINGS FOR TROUBLED TIMES

GOD IS
IN CONTROL

devotions for women

100 READINGS FOR TROUBLED TIMES

GOD IS
IN CONTROL

devotions for women

PAMELA L. MCQUADE

BARBOUR
PUBLISHING

Cover Design by Greg Jackson, Thinkpen Design

Published by Barbour Publishing, Inc., 1810 Barbour Drive, Uhrichsville, Ohio 44683, www.barbourbooks.com

Our mission is to inspire the world with the life-changing message of the Bible.

Member of the
Evangelical Christian
Publishers Association

Printed in China.

INTRODUCTION

Does the craziness of modern society bother you? Does consuming the news, skimming social media, and talking with everyday people leave you frustrated, depressed, even despairing? You can be sure we've all been there at one time or another.

You can also be sure that these feelings are nothing new. When you read God's Word, you'll see that biblical people faced many of the same issues we do. Thousands of years ago, there were personal and family struggles, corrupt political leaders, serious health concerns, and the terrorizing threats of enemies.

Yet the consistent message of scripture is that God is in control. He's aware of and working through every circumstance, even the worst crises humanity can experience. Of course, many of those crises are of our own creation.

Famed nineteenth-century British preacher Charles Spurgeon highlighted a somewhat-obscure scripture that pulls the curtain back to expose God's behind-the-scenes work in human lives. When the nation of Israel divided into two rival countries due to the foolish arrogance of Solomon's son Rehoboam, this new king wanted his army to invade and punish the seceding north. But God told His prophet:

> *"Speak to Rehoboam the son of Solomon, king of Judah, and to all the house of Judah and Benjamin, and to the remnant of the people, saying, 'This is what the LORD says:*

"You shall not go up or fight against your brothers, the children of Israel. Return, every man to his house, for this thing is from Me."'"

1 KINGS 12:23–24 SKJV

It was Rehoboam's cocky, rude answer to the people's request for leniency that had created the national split—but God declared, "This thing is from Me." In response, Spurgeon said, "I believe in the free agency of men, in their responsibility and wickedness, and that everything evil comes of them, but I also believe in God, that 'this thing' which, on the one side of it, was purely and alone from men, on another side of it was still from God who rules both evil and good, and not only walks the garden of Eden in the cool of a summer's eve, but walks the billows of the tempestuous sea, and rules everywhere by His sovereign might."

When you look for them, you'll find dozens of biblical cases where God was indeed working His will through people's difficult circumstances. The one hundred devotions in this book will help you see the unseen—the hand of God in every occurrence of life—and encourage you with the truth of His knowledge and power.

Never forget what the apostle Paul taught—that for those who love God, "we know that all things work together for good" (Romans 8:28 SKJV). That's true because *God* is the one doing the work.

WHOOPEE?

"Listen to this, Job; stop and consider God's wonders. Do you know how God controls the clouds and makes his lightning flash?"

JOB 37:14–15 NIV

When we hear the words *God is in control*, we may not shout, "Whoopee!"

That's because we have mixed emotions about the idea. Some days, when our backs are to the wall and God rescues us, it may seem like a truth to rejoice in. A shout of praise may be the first word from our lips. But at other times, when we still think we can work things out on our own, we might feel a little less certain.

Job's back was hard against the wall. Just about every awful thing that could happen had come into his life. He'd lost his children and almost everything he owned. His health had deteriorated. His wife turned against him and told him to die. His friends insisted he had done something wrong and God was mad at him.

Job's suffering didn't end quickly. But he remained faithful. And finally God responded to Job's irritating and seemingly heartless friends, like Elihu, who spoke these words in Job 37.

Elihu's timing and compassion were all off. When Job needed comfort, self-righteous Elihu condemned. But in a warped kind of way, Elihu had it right. God *was* greater than Job, and He was in control of things Job had no clue about. When the perfect God confronted Job with these truths, the pained man heard and heeded—and he repented. Then there might have been an unspoken "whoopee" in Job's heart. God would restore him—that's what He'd had in mind all along, once Job admitted that God was God and Job was not.

It's hard for us to admit we don't have control and God does. Our sin-filled hearts resist admitting our own limitations. But, like Job, we eventually find that resistance gets us nowhere. Accepting God's rule over our lives and looking to Him in all things is to experience the "whoopee" in life. For with Him is pure joy on earth and in eternity!

LORD, I WANT YOU TO CONTROL MY LIFE. FORGIVE ME FOR GRABBING AT POWER WHEN I NEED TO HAND IT TO YOU.

THE LONG VIEW

Whatever is has already been, and what will be has been before; and God will call the past to account.

When life is going less than perfectly (isn't that many days in this imperfect world?), our nerves may get strained and we may feel tempted to doubt. Injustices seem to go on unquestioned, and wrongdoing never gets punished.

The world can seem like a miserable place, especially on our most troubled days. We may begin to wonder if God has stepped out of the picture.

But before we give in to doubt, let's remember to take the long view. God doesn't always jump in and correct wrongs in a moment. That doesn't mean evil will win in the end or even that our personal lives will always be messy. If we've read the New Testament, we know that God sent His Son to bring justice in the end and to set up His rule, destroying evil. Satan and his minions will eventually receive their just deserts, and God will rule. That's the end of the story, the end we put our hope in.

Just as He deals with evil and awfulness on a large scale, God deals with the messy bits of our lives. He may call us to account for our own sins and make things right. If we've been careless, we may have to reorganize our finances and begin to pay off our debts. We may need to work on our relationships or forgive a serious wrong. Working with God, we can find solutions to almost any problem.

On those days when evil still feels overwhelming, let's remember that God has dealt with situations like this before. We are not the only ones to experience injustice or troubles. Ecclesiastes 1:9 (skjv) tells us, "There is nothing new under the sun." Some Christian somewhere has faced a situation like ours, and God has been faithful to that person. He will be faithful to us too.

LORD, HELP ME WHEN I AM TEMPTED TO DOUBT.
FORGIVE ME FOR MY FAITHLESSNESS AND
DRAW ME NEARER TO YOU IN FAITH.

NEVER SLIPPING

So when the Ishmaelites, who were Midianite
traders, came by, Joseph's brothers pulled him out of
the cistern and sold him to them for twenty pieces
of silver. And the traders took him to Egypt.
GENESIS 37:28 NLT

Talk about bad days. For Joseph, this was the worst. If someone
had told Joseph that this miserable day would lead to wonderful things, he might have thought that person was crazy. How
could being hauled up out of the cistern where his brothers
had thrown him, watching his brothers accept money for him,
and being dragged off to Egypt be the start of anything good?

We aren't surprised at the idea that Joseph probably felt
discouraged. It's natural not to rush to see the good things in
miserable situations.

But that's only if we remove God from the picture. God had
a plan, and it wasn't one that left Joseph in miserable slavery.

Joseph was hauled into a strange land, had to learn a different language to communicate with anyone, and was put to
work as a household servant. Doubtless his first tasks were less
than interesting, but his master, Potiphar, saw Joseph's worth
and moved him into better work.

Eventually, despite his trials, which included time in jail after being falsely accused of rape, Joseph came to the attention of Pharaoh—and ended up being the second-most-powerful man in the land.

All that came out of the miserable day when Joseph's brothers betrayed him!

Like Joseph, we must never give up and never lose faith, no matter how little we recognize of God's control—or how little of His favor we seem to gain. Until the story ends, we cannot understand God's plan or purpose. Some things we may never comprehend in this world, yet we can trust that eternity's view will be a much better one.

Nothing slips out of God's hands—most especially not His children.

LORD, I THANK YOU THAT I AM YOUR CHILD AND THAT
YOU NEVER LET ME SLIP BETWEEN YOUR FINGERS.
THANK YOU FOR BEING IN CONTROL OF MY WHOLE LIFE.

DAWNING HOPE

And we know that God causes everything to work
together for the good of those who love God and
are called according to his purpose for them.
ROMANS 8:28 NLT

When life is going well, when our relationships are happy, when we're satisfied in our jobs, when our loved ones are thriving, we probably don't question whether God is in control.

Good things always come from God, and we tend to assume that we deserve a peaceful, happy life. Peaceful lives, we tell ourselves, are godly lives. If life is happy, we assume God approves of us and life is the way it's supposed to be. Only when life becomes stressful, when troubles hit us, do we start questioning God's power and even His love for us.

Yet God never promises us a life of ease. What He does promise is even better: "For our present troubles are small and won't last very long. Yet they produce for us a glory that vastly outweighs them and will last forever!" (2 Corinthians 4:17 NLT). Anything that troubles us is small, ephemeral stuff. Though it may feel as if pain will last forever, it simply can't.

Even the very bad stuff ends up being something we can thank God for. When we worship Him in heaven, we will praise Him that whatever we faced on earth never separated us from Him.

The things we call "bad" may feel that way because they make us recognize our own painful sin. Though they feel negative, in the end these trials push us away from sin and into the arms of Jesus.

Even if we cannot see the good, God can. Instead of opening ourselves to doubt and fear, let's draw close to Him in trust that this too will bring about our good and His glory. As we see ourselves through His eyes, hope will dawn again.

HELP ME TO SEE MY TROUBLES THROUGH YOUR EYES, LORD. BRING TRUST AND HOPE INTO MY HEART.

CALLED?

I pray that your hearts will be flooded with light so that you can understand the confident hope he has given to those he called— his holy people who are his rich and glorious inheritance.
EPHESIANS 1:18 NLT

Which people find that everything always works for their good?

"Those who love God and are called according to his purpose for them" (Romans 8:28 NLT). They are the ones God calls—those who have experienced the hope He offers to all who will believe in Him.

Some people would like to believe that God shuttles everyone into heaven, no matter what they believe. But that's not a biblical view of God or faith. God does not want anyone to perish (2 Peter 3:9), but all people have sinned and fall short of His glory (Romans 3:23).

Yet our merciful God, who is still in control, chose not to give up on the human race. Instead of condemning us for our sin, He made a way of salvation, sending His Son as a sacrifice to reconcile fallen humanity to Himself. "When we were still without strength, in due time Christ died for the ungodly. . . . God demonstrates His love toward us, in that while we were still sinners, Christ died for us" (Romans 5:6, 8 SKJV).

Those who accept that sacrifice and believe in Him are the ones He has called, His holy people. They have heard His call to faith and answered, "Yes, I have sinned. I need You, Jesus. Forgive me for my sins. I want to walk in Your ways." In that very moment they became His valuable inheritance.

God is in control. Even from the moment when the first sinners, Adam and Eve, fell, He planned a path of forgiveness. Have you walked down it?

LORD, THANK YOU THAT EVEN SIN COULD NOT RIP CONTROL FROM YOUR HANDS. THANK YOU FOR OFFERING ME FORGIVENESS. I PLACE MY SIN BEFORE YOU AND ASK YOU TO CLEANSE MY HEART AND MAKE ME WHOLE IN YOU.

UNREVOKED PROMISE

"Do not fear, for I have redeemed you. I have called you by your name. You are Mine. When you pass through the waters, I will be with you, and through the rivers, they shall not overflow you. When you walk through the fire, you shall not be burned, nor shall the flame kindle on you."

Isaiah 43:1–2 skjv

. . . .

In the eighth century BC, the people of Judah felt as if they lived on a knife edge. They had faced war with the northern kingdom of Israel and her allies. Then Assyria attacked Judah and moved south to lay siege to Jerusalem. Eventually Judah ended up being conquered by the Babylonian empire. Most of the people were carried off to this strange pagan nation.

What did God say to His people in this situation? First, He reminded them of the past. He had called them by name; He knew just who they were. Despite the faithlessness of the people He covenanted with, He still called them "Mine." They may have deserted Him, but God had not left them. They still had a future with Him.

No matter if they feel overwhelmed by a flood or about to be burned by flames, no earthly danger will overwhelm God's people. God meant that when He spoke to the people of Judah.

It is a promise He never revoked, and it applies to those who trust in His Son.

Are you having one of those days when you wonder if you will be washed away by a flood or burned in flames? Remember your calling and God's faithfulness. Just as the people of Judah returned to their home, centuries ago, you too can expect a future of better things. God is always faithful. In the end, every true believer comes home to heaven.

In the meantime, confess any sin, draw close to God, and delight in the blessings He has in store for you here. The best ones may be just around the corner.

LORD, ON HARD DAYS, HELP ME REMEMBER THAT YOU HAVE CALLED ME AND THAT YOU ARE *ALWAYS* FAITHFUL. YOU HAVE COMMITTED TO ME AND WILL NEVER GIVE UP ON ME. THANK YOU.

DEADLY ENEMY?

And thus when He had spoken, He cried with a loud voice, "Lazarus, come out!" And he who was dead came out, bound hand and foot with grave clothes, and his face was bound about with a cloth. Jesus said to them, "Unbind him, and let him go."

JOHN 11:43–44 SKJV

Death is our most-feared enemy. Though we shove it to the back of our minds for most of our lives, it pokes its head up at the worst moments. And ultimately, it's the one thing we cannot avoid.

When death stares us in the face, we look away. Our power over it is nonexistent. The pain it causes tears our hearts apart. Deep down we know this was never the way God made things to be.

With His resurrection, Jesus overcame death, providing us with a way to eternal life. Before that, the most powerful picture of His control over death had been the raising of Lazarus.

One day, God's power will again demonstrate that Satan and his deeds do not have the last say. Though death may seem to control us now, scripture repeatedly promises that Satan will be overcome.

We may grieve the loss of family and friends who are as close as family. We may sorrow for the loss of many. But those who know Jesus live in the certainty that God has not yet spoken His last word. And that's not because He couldn't restore people to earthly life immediately but because He has a plan for an even better life in eternity for those who know Him.

Death may seem to control the world now, but a day will come when "death is swallowed up in victory" (1 Corinthians 15:54 SKJV). At the sound of the last trumpet, the final resurrection will make Lazarus' temporary return to life look like small potatoes.

One day, we will share eternal life with Jesus.

LORD, WHEN I GRIEVE OVER A DEATH,
REMIND ME THAT YOU WILL ONE DAY SAY THE LAST
WORD, AND WE WILL BE WITH YOU IN ETERNITY.
HELP ME TO BE FAITHFUL UNTIL THAT DAY.

BEST BATTLE PLAN

*Some trust in chariots and some in horses, but we
trust in the name of the LORD our God.*
PSALM 20:7 NIV

Horses and chariots were the high-tech weaponry of David's day. Well-made chariots and highly trained battle steeds could help warriors take down many troops. Essentially the chariot was a moving platform men could stand on and effectively rain down arrows or spears on foot soldiers below them. It's not surprising that commanders put their trust in these.

But David knew what he spoke of when he maintained that putting faith in men, their mounts, and those wheeled carts was a losing proposition. Compared to these, God's power made the enemy's best men and machines look like tiny toys.

David watched God's wise battle plan and His strength sweep away every enemy advantage as he fought with King Saul. The David of "David and Goliath"—a vulnerable boy who faced a powerful, hardened warrior—had a history of achieving victory because his trust was in his God, not in armor, swords, or other accoutrements of warfare.

Most of us are not involved in warfare. We certainly don't use the weapons of David's era. Nor can we learn much from his enemies. But for spiritual warfare, David's battle plan is as valuable today as it was in his day.

David's victories came because he trusted in God, not his own abilities or even those of his men. He knew God was in control, and he banked his future on it. With that faith, he became the ruler of a nation and encouraged his people to trust in the God who brought him victory. As he lived by faith, David successfully overcame many trials.

Does God control our lives, or do we look elsewhere for strength? The horses and chariots of our world will only let us down.

LORD, HELP ME RECOGNIZE THAT YOU MUST CONTROL MY LIFE. HELP ME TO TURN ASIDE FROM WORLDLY THINGS AND TRUST IN YOU.

SAFE IN GOD'S HANDS

So it came to pass, when the king's commandment and decree were heard, and when many young women were gathered together to Susa the palace, to the custody of Hegai, that Esther was brought also to the king's house, to the custody of Hegai, keeper of the women.
ESTHER 2:8 SKJV

As all the most beautiful women of King Ahasuerus' nation were herded into his harem, Esther was swept up among them.

Imagine how terrifying that must have been. She was one of many, headed into the arms of a harsh and powerful king. The whole country had seen how badly he treated his last wife. Stress must have filled Esther's being as she walked into the harem.

But even in this very pagan environment, with a king who wanted to test out all the best-looking women in his kingdom, God gave Esther a powerful appeal. Esther 2:15 (SKJV) reports: "Esther obtained favor in the sight of all those who saw her." Eventually, Ahasuerus decided to make her his queen. The unfamiliar court politics that followed could have undone Esther had God not been with her.

Are you in a terrifying position in your life? Do other forces seem to be in control? Look at Esther. She didn't dare tell the king her greatest secret: she was Jewish. But even when this truth came to light, in a moment when she was forced to save her people, God remained in control. From the moment she was brought into the harem, He had been working out a plan and protecting her.

No threat from man overcomes God's protection. Though Esther must have had hours and even days of stress, she could relax when she acknowledged how firmly God had her in His hands. Though her faith had been tested, she was never truly in danger as she held on to her Lord.

You, too, are held safe in the Lord's hands. *Nothing* can snatch you from His hands.

EVEN WHEN OTHERS SEEM SO POWERFUL, I KNOW THEY HAVE NOTHING LIKE YOUR AUTHORITY, LORD. THANK YOU FOR KEEPING ME SAFE, NO MATTER WHAT I FACE IN LIFE.

PROBLEM SOLVED

*Jesus went with his disciples to the village of Nain,
and a large crowd followed him. A funeral procession
was coming out as he approached the village gate.
The young man who had died was a widow's only son,
and a large crowd from the village was with her.*
LUKE 7:11–12 NLT

Being a widow in ancient Israel wasn't a positive thing. Though scripture encouraged Jews to be generous to widows, it was an uncertain lifestyle. So when this woman's only son died, she knew she had lost her most reliable source of aid. The community support the widow received that day was probably encouraging, but how many people would remember her when she had to pay the bills? Who would care for her when she was old and frail?

But the funeral wasn't the end of the story. Just when the widow of Nain needed Him, Jesus arrived at the widow's town. He could hardly miss the funeral procession coming out of the village gate as He and His disciples approached it. "His heart overflowed with compassion" (Luke 7:13 NLT). He walked over to the coffin, touched it, and told the young man to get up.

The young man rose, brought back to life by that touch. Problem solved.

Do you have a problem that seems to have no solution? Be assured that Jesus has compassion for you and your problem, just as He cared about the poor widow of Nain. He is never as distant as you may sometimes feel He is.

Faith is not a matter of feelings. We may become discouraged and doubtful and wonder where God is amid troubles. Psalm 9:9 (NLT) promises: "The LORD is a shelter for the oppressed, a refuge in times of trouble." When fear and doubt seek to oppress us, God cares for us tenderly. If He feels distant, it may be that our doubts have distanced us in the very moment when He wants to hold us near.

Jesus is ready to walk into your life today. Will you welcome Him?

LORD, THANK YOU FOR CARING FOR ME, NO MATTER
WHAT MY TROUBLES ARE. EVICT DOUBTS FROM
MY HEART AND COME INTO MY LIFE TODAY.

WHO RULES?

*"While these words were still in his mouth, a voice called
down from heaven, 'O King Nebuchadnezzar, this message
is for you! You are no longer ruler of this kingdom. You will
be driven from human society. You will live in the fields
with the wild animals, and you will eat grass like a cow.
Seven periods of time will pass while you live this way,
until you learn that the Most High rules over the kingdoms
of the world and gives them to anyone he chooses.'"*
DANIEL 4:31–32 NLT

King Nebuchadnezzar thought he ruled everything. One day,
as he walked on the roof of his palace and saw the wonderful
buildings that had gone up at his command, he began to boast.

Those were the last words from his mouth for "seven periods of time." We may not know exactly how many days or
even years the king was insane, but it was long enough for the
proud king to learn his lesson that God, not Nebuchadnezzar,
ruled the world.

Looking at worldly powers, we may be tempted to feel that
they *will* last forever. The sins of some leaders appear to influence
our world endlessly. Our hearts grieve as we compare them to
the biblical standards that God calls all people to live by.

Before falling into despair, let's remember that no ruler has power apart from God. Each rules under His command, even those who do not recognize Him. God determines the extent of each leader's power and can step in to limit it, as He did with the Babylonian king.

God calls us to pray for our country's leaders, even those we don't approve of. Some seem to drive us to prayer more than others, but that's all to the good. We need to spend time bringing our world before the Holy One. Even our best leaders are frail. The worst of them need us to run to God even more. Then the benefit of our prayers might be seen throughout our land.

LORD, KEEP ME IN DAILY PRAYER FOR OUR
COUNTRY'S LEADERS. AND REMIND ME THAT MY
VISION FOR OUR LAND MAY NOT BE YOURS.

NO CHANCE!

And when she could no longer hide him, she took an
ark of bulrushes for him, and covered it with slime
and with pitch, and put the child in it. And she laid
it in the reeds by the river's bank. And his sister stood
afar off, to know what would be done to him.

EXODUS 2:3–4 SKJV

Imagine having to take your child and float him in a tiny, handmade boat on the Nile River. How easily could it be tipped over? What wild creature could attack him? And only his young sister would be there to intervene.

Today, such a parent could be accused of child endangerment. But there was no one in Egypt to care about this boy. Pharaoh had condemned all Hebrew boys to death. Floating their baby boy in a fragile boat in the reeds was the only way this child's parents could hope to keep him alive. It was not lack of love or sense that brought them to do this.

Pharaoh's kindhearted daughter found and protected the child, whom she named Moses. The boy's sister offered to find a nurse for him—their own mother.

After Moses grew, he became part of the royal household, a place where he would learn how the palace and politics worked.

Understanding these became part of the job God had in mind for him, many years in the future. The boy who almost didn't live became God's prophet and the man who would lead the Hebrews out of slavery into freedom.

All the details of Moses' life, even the scary ones, were fine-tuned to become part of the larger plan for God's people. Nothing was left to chance. There was no chance about it, with God in charge.

Is there chance in our lives? No. For the God who prepared each detail of Moses' life has ours in His hands too. What may seem like chance or happenstance is no such thing. Chance just doesn't exist when God controls a life.

LORD, I THANK YOU THAT NOTHING UNEXPECTED
CAN COME INTO MY LIFE. EVEN IF I DON'T EXPECT IT,
YOU KNOW THE WHOLE COURSE OF MY LIFE. HELP
ME TO TRUST IN YOU, WHEREVER THAT GOES.

THAT OTHER NEIGHBOR

*"You have heard the law that says, 'Love your neighbor'
and hate your enemy. But I say, love your enemies!
Pray for those who persecute you! In that way, you will
be acting as true children of your Father in heaven.
For he gives his sunlight to both the evil and the good,
and he sends rain on the just and the unjust alike."*

MATTHEW 5:43–45 NLT

Sometimes, loving your neighbor is a piece of cake. Great people you enjoy living near are easy to love.

But then there are the other kind of neighbors, who find just the right buttons to push and push them often. Maybe they throw loud parties or don't keep up their property or—worst of all—take advantage of you and your family.

God doesn't say, "Love the neighbors who are easy to love." After all, He loves even the wrongdoers on this earth and sends His provision into their lives as much as He sends it to yours. People's irritating or even wicked attitudes don't stop God's love.

Now for the difficult bit: just as the Lord loves the unlovable, He expects His people to follow His example. After all, He loved us before we heard His call to follow Him. And He wants us to be just like Him.

Where do we start showing this love? Hard feelings may make it impossible to have much of a relationship with a nasty neighbor. So God doesn't ask us to start with a face-to-face confrontation. He asks us to pray for them in our homes in our quiet time with Him. Prayer not only changes the person we pray for; it changes us. And no matter how much we think we are in the right and our neighbors are wrong, we may be mistaken. God has the answers for all our broken relationships, but we must accept His answers.

Then we need to trust God for the outcome. He who controls the heavens and the earth also controls our little property.

Let's come to God, and as Martin Luther said, "Pray, and let God worry."

LORD, I ASK YOU TO GIVE PEACE TO ME
AND MY NEIGHBORS. MAY I PRAY FOR THEM
REGULARLY AND CARE FOR THEM TOO.

PREPARED

"Or who closed up the sea with doors when it broke forth as if it had flowed out of the womb. . .and said, 'This far you shall come, but no farther, and here your proud waves shall stop'?"

JOB 38:8, 11 SKJV

If you live near the shore and a hurricane is coming, you become immediately aware of the power of the ocean. Terror may strike your heart.

It makes sense to prepare for dangers. If you live in a hurricane-prone area, you need to have a plan.

But not all dangers are predictable. Job could never have known what troubles would come into his life in just a moment.

That didn't mean he wasn't prepared though. Job had spent a lifetime making sure he and his family followed God. Job made certain his family never neglected the proper sacrifices, even for sins they were unaware of. Certainly, he did the same for his own wrongs too.

Job's preparedness didn't keep the troubles at bay, but when his wife told him to give up and die and his friends insisted he was hiding some terrible sin, Job knew the truth. He may not have understood God completely, but neither did he give up or lose faith.

Job had reason not to give up. The God he worshiped wasn't an idol who could not lift a hand to help him. God had a purpose in Job's suffering, and in the end Job recognized the greatness of God and his own severe limitations.

We are limited in our ability to face life's storms. Do we recognize that the God who controls the seas oversees our lives, no matter how messed up they are? Just as He controls the most powerful elements of the earth, with one wave of the hand He could remove every storm from our lives. If He doesn't, let's consider His power over the sea and understand that the forces we face in our lives also have a purpose in His plan.

LORD, I MAY NOT APPRECIATE HAVING TRIALS IN MY LIFE, BUT I KNOW THAT EVEN THESE ARE NOT BEYOND YOUR CONTROL. HELP ME TRUST THAT NOTHING COMES INTO MY LIFE THAT IS NOT FROM YOUR HAND.

STILL IN CHARGE

Daniel answered and said, "Blessed be the name of God forever and ever, for wisdom and might are His. And He changes the times and the seasons. He removes kings and sets up kings. He gives wisdom to the wise and knowledge to those who know understanding."
DANIEL 2:20–21 SKJV

Most of us don't live in a land where kings rule, but we understand that kings historically had power that seemed limitless and overwhelming. Daniel lived in an age of a tyrant king. He couldn't change the system, especially as a member of a conquered people. Yet God used him powerfully within the political system of his time.

Daniel served King Nebuchadnezzar, not because this was his preferred ruler or job but because he had no choice. The Babylonian system of government probably wasn't one he would have voted for, even if he could have. Yet no matter where he was, the prophet would serve God and provide His wisdom to those who needed it.

The world may not understand our desire to live in a godly country. It may decry our ideals. Politics often becomes very ungodly. No matter how powerful it is, though, no political machine is ultimately in control. People set up political systems, but they can never fully depose God as king. Even those who do not recognize His existence or authority cannot fully escape the rule of the always-sovereign King.

Inside a corrupt political system, God may have a few faithful people who try to bring His truth to light. They may seem powerless, until the moment when God puts them center stage or uses them to bring His will to pass. Even leaders who do not know Him may become pawns in God's game plan.

Though everything seems to be going wrong indeed, we can trust that God is still in charge and will bring His will to pass.

LORD, I TRUST THAT YOU ARE STILL IN CHARGE.
KEEP ME FAITHFUL IN SERVING YOU, NO
MATTER HOW GRIM THINGS LOOK.

SLIM CHANCE?

*Now, therefore, Tattenai, governor beyond the river,
Shethar-boz-enai, and your companions the Apharsachites,
who are beyond the river, stay far from there. Leave the work
of this house of God alone. Let the governor of the Jews and
the elders of the Jews build this house of God in its place.*
EZRA 6:6–7 SKJV

King Cyrus had granted the Jews the right to return to their land and rebuild the temple. But officious Tattenai, governor of the province, barged in on the Jews' efforts and demanded to know what right they had to work. Evidently, he hadn't gotten the memo. The fearful governor, who thought the Jews planned to rebel, held up their efforts while he contacted the new king, Darius.

Because of this lack of communication and change in staff, the temple building could not go on. But as the question of the right to rebuild worked its way through official channels, the documentation was eventually uncovered. The king wrote to his governor and commanded that the work begin again.

When the issue came before the king, a favorable result hadn't seemed likely. The governor was accusing the Jews of sedition—and it was true that before they were conquered and sent to Babylon, many had fought tooth and nail for their freedom. But that was not their plan now.

At first, Darius ordered a stop. But the court scribes found records showing that Cyrus had indeed given the Jews authority to rebuild. God had worked on the previous king's heart, and this new king acceded to his plan. So building restarted.

We may find ourselves opposed by powers beyond our control, and we know how those ancient Jews felt. Time inches by as we await a resolution. Though we may be certain we are in the right, nothing is decided quickly.

We may think our chances of success are slim. But we must not discount God's authority and power. In His mercy, God may bring us a more positive outcome than we expect.

Never give up.

LORD, HELP ME TO STAND FIRM IN FAITH THAT YOU,
NOT ANY HUMAN BEING OR INSTITUTION, CONTROL MY LIFE.

MASTER PLAN

At that time the Roman emperor, Augustus, decreed that a census should be taken throughout the Roman Empire. . . . All returned to their own ancestral towns to register for this census. And because Joseph was a descendant of King David, he had to go to Bethlehem in Judea, David's ancient home. He traveled there from the village of Nazareth in Galilee.

Luke 2:1, 3–4 NLT

. . . .

When Augustus decreed that a census should be taken, he was doing it for political reasons. He wasn't thinking about the contentious nation of Israel. Certainly, he had no thoughts about a ruler sent by God; he would have seen that as a threat to his own power.

Yet that census fulfilled a prophecy: "But you, O Bethlehem Ephrathah, are only a small village among all the people of Judah. Yet a ruler of Israel, whose origins are in the distant past, will come from you on my behalf" (Micah 5:2 NLT). An emperor's command sent Mary and Joseph on a ninety-five-mile journey so that Jesus, the promised Messiah, would be born in the prophesied village.

That village would not have stood out in its day as being important. People were not clamoring to have their child born there. Yet this was the place God chose for the birth of His Son, and He'd shared that information with Micah. No one who claimed to be God's Messiah could be born anywhere else.

Augustus had no clue that God was using him for a divine plan. Yet a command that disrupted the whole empire was fine-tuned to God's purpose.

Augustus wasn't the only one who was part of that plan. Joseph "just happened" to come from Bethlehem? Not really. God had that piece of the plan in place long before Augustus thought of a census. And Joseph was also in place in Nazareth, where he met Mary and became betrothed to her.

God's a master at making detailed plans. He did it over two thousand years ago, and He does it for us today too. Have you seen and appreciated His plan in your life?

LORD, THANK YOU FOR HAVING A
DETAILED PLAN FOR MY LIFE.

NEVER DESPERATE

A woman in the crowd had suffered for twelve years with constant bleeding. She had suffered a great deal from many doctors, and over the years she had spent everything she had to pay them, but she had gotten no better. In fact, she had gotten worse.

<small>MARK 5:25–26 NLT</small>

Can't you feel for this woman? Not only had she suffered from an irritating, messy, and possibly painful health issue, but it made her ritually unclean. No one could touch her without also becoming unclean, so she probably hadn't had so much as a hug in a long time. She'd gone from doctor to doctor, and none could cure her. Everything simply got worse.

Frustration filled her life, and now she was poor. She'd done nothing wrong, yet her life had many burdens.

Finally, she heard that Jesus was in town, and she took a last step, barely hopeful that even He could help.

Knowing that her touch would make Jesus unclean, she crept up behind Him and dared not touch His person. "If I can just touch his robe, I will be healed," she thought (Mark 5:28 NLT).

It's no wonder, considering everything she'd been through, that she had doubts. Why would He want to have anything to do with her? After all, everyone else avoided her.

When we face seemingly insurmountable odds, we may relate to this nameless woman. Nothing seems to be going for us. We feel as if no one cares. Then Satan whispers in our ears, "Not even God cares about your troubles."

Nothing could be less true. But if we give up on God and refuse to approach Him, we will never know that. When we don't grab on to enough courage to touch His robe, our own disillusionment keeps us from knowing how deeply He cares.

The moment she touched His robe, the woman knew she was healed. For us, it may take a bit longer, but we can know that our troubles are in the hands of Jesus and that He brings healing of body, heart, and soul. We need never be desperate.

LORD JESUS, THANK YOU FOR CARING FOR ME,
EVEN WHEN I FEEL DESPERATE. IN YOU I NEVER TRULY AM.

SMALL THINGS

*One day as Mordecai was on duty at the king's gate,
two of the king's eunuchs, Bigthana and Teresh—who were
guards at the door of the king's private quarters—became
angry at King Xerxes and plotted to assassinate him.*

ESTHER 2:21 NLT

Okay, so Bigthana and Teresh weren't the brightest conspirators. They didn't sneak away to a private place to hatch their plot against King Xerxes. In their anger, they spoke publicly and loudly enough that Queen Esther's cousin Mordecai could overhear their plans. The highly trusted guards were no longer faithful to Xerxes, and the king's life was endangered.

Our omnipotent God put the queen's cousin in just the right place at just the right time to overhear the danger to the king. And faithful Mordecai didn't ignore what he'd heard. Instead, he reported it to Queen Esther, who told the king. Ultimately, the ones who lost their lives were the plotting guards.

How many times does our all-powerful God put us in just the right place at just the time when He needs us to do something? We may be with an unsaved friend who needs comfort and tell her of His love. If she believes in Jesus as a result, being in the right place just then has become a heavenly opportunity.

We may not change a political situation, as Mordecai did, but we will have partnered with God in saving a soul. And who knows what that other soul may accomplish for God's kingdom?

Many of the "coincidences" that come our way are placed in our lives by God. It is up to us to use them wisely. Even things that seem to have no great spiritual value may be used well in God's hands. When Mordecai told of the threat to Xerxes, it probably seemed like another day at the office. Little did the queen's cousin know it would eventually lead to his being put in a position of trust in the court, where he could do God's work more broadly.

When we are faithful in the small things, God can give us bigger things to do for Him too.

LORD, HELP ME TO BE FAITHFUL IN SMALL
THINGS, TO BRING GLORY TO YOU.

EVERY DAY OF MY LIFE

And Isaac entreated the LORD for his wife because she was barren, and the LORD was entreated by him, and Rebekah his wife conceived. And the children struggled together within her, and she said, "If it is so, why am I thus?" And she went to inquire of the LORD. And the LORD said to her, "Two nations are in your womb, and two kinds of people shall be separated from your body, and the one people shall be stronger than the other people, and the elder shall serve the younger."

GENESIS 25:21–23 SKJV

. . . .

After waiting a long time to become pregnant, Rebekah felt as if she had a war within her womb. What was going on?

Rebekah asked God this question, and He answered. The two boys would form two nations. The younger would be stronger than the elder, and their disagreements had started even before their birth.

From the moment of their conception, Esau and Jacob were different. Their life paths had already been set. Esau was the elder, a hunter, and his father's favorite, while Jacob was a quieter sort and his mother's favorite. But God foresaw their ending and had foretold that Esau would serve his brother.

The sportsman sold his birthright to the quiet, opportunistic son. Esau would never forget that moment. Though he freely made the choice to sell his future cheaply, for many years—if not for his whole life—he would blame his brother for the decision. In his heart, Esau wanted to kill his brother.

Though the brothers eventually came to some sort of peace, Esau's nation of Edom never became as great as Israel, and the two countries remained enemies.

Psalm 139:16 (NLT) says, "You saw me before I was born. Every day of my life was recorded in your book. Every moment was laid out before a single day had passed." God knows all the events of our lives before they happen. That doesn't mean we cannot make choices, but He knows the challenges we will face and the decisions we will make.

If we daily seek God's will, our lives can consistently please Him.

LORD, I WANT TO DO YOUR WILL EACH DAY.
SHOW ME HOW TO PLEASE YOU TODAY.

FAITHFUL GLEANING

So Ruth went out to gather grain behind the harvesters.
And as it happened, she found herself working in a field that
belonged to Boaz, the relative of her father-in-law, Elimelech.
RUTH 2:3 NLT

Ruth and Naomi left Moab and returned to Naomi's homeland, Israel. Their husbands had died, and they were in a difficult situation. Yet Ruth had refused to desert her mother-in-law and return to her own family, who probably would have found her a new husband. Together, the women walked to Naomi's homeland.

When they got there, Ruth volunteered to work for their living by gathering grain. Jewish law said reapers should not collect every bit of the harvest but leave grain on the edges of the field for the poor to gather (Leviticus 23:22).

The landowner, Boaz, had heard of Ruth's generous offer to stay with Naomi. When he found she was in his field and learned how industrious she was, he commanded his servants to look after her and allow her to drink some of their water. He provided her with a meal and leftovers too. Then he told his harvesters to leave extra grain for her to gather. At the end of the day, Ruth had gathered a substantial amount of food.

When Naomi discovered it was Boaz's field Ruth had gleaned, she recognized him as a relative who could redeem them from their poverty. And he did.

As the women relied on God to care for them, Ruth "chanced on" Boaz's field. But there was no chance about it. God had an immediate plan for Ruth and Boaz. They would marry, and Naomi's situation would again be secure. Yet God also had a greater long-term plan: Boaz and Ruth would have a son, Obed, who would be King David's grandfather. From David's line came Jesus, the Messiah. Many unexpected blessings came to one humble woman who faithfully gleaned a field.

LORD, HELP ME TO FAITHFULLY GLEAN WHATEVER FIELD YOU PUT ME IN. THEN I KNOW I WILL BE BLESSED.

ALIGNED WITH GOD

"For in Him we live and move and have our being, as also some of your own poets have said, 'For we are also His offspring.'"
ACTS 17:28 SKJV

Worshiping the God who is in control of everything may seem a bit intimidating at times. When we look at His power and authority, we can feel overwhelmed.

But we feel that only until we recognize our connection with this powerful being. We may wonder that He—the one who controls all that goes on in all of creation—would have anything to do with us. But our fears abate as we realize the blessing He offers us—to be connected to Him, not simply as people who know about Him, but as His daughters. We are His much-loved and cared-for children, whom He has called into relationship with Himself.

When we relate to Him in love, we no longer need to fear His power. Jesus has taken the judgment we as sinners deserved. The Mighty One doesn't seek to destroy or punish us. Instead, God's love is poured out on us, and He offers us the power of His Spirit at work in our lives. His love toward us makes His power benevolent.

God may redirect our lives if we stray. We may face challenges that refine our faith. But alignment with God means we rely on His strength in our lives.

We cannot move physical mountains—but then we never could before we knew Him either. But spiritual mountains shift at His command when we pray and act in His will. Troubles that seemed impossible slide out of our lives at His will. And we feel His love redefining our lives.

Are you living in Christ? Does He direct how you live and move and have your being? When He's the center of your life, you need not fear His power. Your world is controlled by the master of the universe.

LORD, I WANT MY LIFE TO ALIGN WITH YOU.
MAY I LIVE EACH DAY IN YOUR POWER, NOT MY OWN.

NO REVENGE

And Joseph said to them, "Do not fear, for am I in
the place of God? But as for you, you thought evil
against me, but God meant it for good, to bring to
pass, as it is this day, to save many people alive."
GENESIS 50:19–20 SKJV

. . . .

When their father died, Joseph's brothers understood their
protection was gone. While Joseph might once have held off
punishing them for selling him into slavery in Egypt, there was
no man to stand in his way now.

The brothers came to Joseph in humility, asking him for
the forgiveness he had already given. And this second-most-
powerful person in the most powerful nation of the Middle
East reassured them that he was not holding a grudge against
them. He could see the good that had come from their terrible
act, and he knew that God's hand had been in it.

Joseph's attitude prefigures the love of Christ. As our Savior
suffered for our sins and never holds them against us, Joseph
put the wickedness of his brothers behind them all and never
sought payback. Even evil against the innocent is not beyond
God's reworking. Joseph's family's salvation from a deadly
famine came about because God had Joseph in the right place

at the right time and gave him preferment in a foreign court.

Our lives also have struggles. But they are never outside of God's ability to rework into good. Relationship mistakes we've made, for example, might lead down a different path of reconciliation. Our part is to seek that reconciliation as much as possible in this world and leave the rest to God.

Just as Joseph did not seek revenge for his brothers' misdeeds, God is never looking for revenge for our sins. When Jesus brought forgiveness, He did not limit it. There was no payback clause in fine print at the bottom of the page. God's power to forgive has no statute of limitations. All He asks of us is confession of our wrongs and willingness to surrender to Him as Lord of our lives. Salvation requires not our perfection but His.

LORD JESUS, THANK YOU FOR SHARING
YOUR PERFECTION WITH ME.

THE PRICE OF
TWO SPARROWS

*"What is the price of two sparrows—one copper coin?
But not a single sparrow can fall to the ground without
your Father knowing it. And the very hairs on your
head are all numbered. So don't be afraid; you are more
valuable to God than a whole flock of sparrows."*
MATTHEW 10:29–31 NLT

The God who set the earth on its axis and flung stars into the sky commands every detail of all creation. Not even a single, seemingly valueless, sparrow falls to earth without the knowledge of the Father.

Nor does any element of our lives fall outside His awesome knowledge. The bad day at the office, the harsh and false words spoken by a friend, the doubts that fill our minds. . .none are new to the Lord who knows just how many hairs are on our heads today and how many will still be there tomorrow. Yet none of our worst minutiae will be used against us. Because we have accepted Jesus' sacrifice and placed our sins on the altar, God is seeking not to punish us with loss but to care for every bit of our lives.

Trusting God with all the details of our lives and admitting the sins that have infiltrated our lives can be daunting. We'd like to have Him think well of us, and our warped sense of righteousness fools us into thinking that not telling God of our failings obscures them from Him.

But Proverbs 28:13 (NLT) tells us, "People who conceal their sins will not prosper, but if they confess and turn from them, they will receive mercy." God offers us mercy, yet we fear that His heart is not tender.

He tries to communicate His love by telling us we are more important to Him than any number of birds on the wing. He knows and cares about each and every one of them. He know and cares about you far more.

LORD, FORGIVE ME FOR TRYING TO HIDE
THINGS YOU ALREADY KNOW. HELP ME TO
TRUST IN YOUR MERCY INSTEAD.

THE DRAMATIC

Elijah stepped forward and prayed: "LORD, the God of Abraham, Isaac and Israel, let it be known today that you are God in Israel and that I am your servant and have done all these things at your command. Answer me, LORD, answer me, so these people will know that you, LORD, are God, and that you are turning their hearts back again." Then the fire of the LORD fell and burned up the sacrifice, the wood, the stones and the soil, and also licked up the water in the trench.

1 KINGS 18:36–38 NIV

The people of Israel, led astray by King Ahab, wandered far from God and worshiped the pagan god Baal. Though God repeatedly tried to get their attention and tell them this was worthless worship, the Israelites continued their rebellion.

After famine destroyed their land for three years, God's prophet Elijah suggested a showdown between Baal and the Lord. Both sides would offer a sacrifice on Mount Carmel. The only thing each side would leave out was the fire that ignited the offering. The real deity would provide that.

The 450 priests of Baal set up their offering and prayed. Nothing happened. They danced around the altar, slashing themselves with swords and spears, trying to get their idol's attention. No response.

Elijah left nothing to chance. He carefully rebuilt the Lord's altar and set up the offering. He had men pour twelve large jars of water over it until all was soaked. Then Elijah simply prayed. God's fire fell and burned up everything—even licking up the water pooled around the altar. Suddenly, the people knew who God was. They couldn't deny His power. And the famine ended with the rain God sent.

God can act with dramatic power, but He doesn't often do it. Perhaps that's because He doesn't want us always wanting the dramatic instead of seeking to know Him. But even in the quiet times, He is there. He is active.

Has God done something dramatic in your life? Whether or not He has, recognize that the methods God uses are not the important thing. Every day is not a Mount Carmel moment, but every day you seek Him is blessed.

Are you seeking Him now?

LORD, EVEN ON ORDINARY DAYS,
PLEASE CONTROL MY LIFE.

HEART SACRIFICE

It was by faith that Abraham offered Isaac as a sacrifice when God was testing him. Abraham, who had received God's promises, was ready to sacrifice his only son, Isaac, even though God had told him, "Isaac is the son through whom your descendants will be counted." Abraham reasoned that if Isaac died, God was able to bring him back to life again. And in a sense, Abraham did receive his son back from the dead.

Hebrews 11:17–19 nlt

Abraham trusted that God was in control—so much so that he was willing to place his son's life in God's hands.

Anyone who has had a seriously ill loved one knows what a challenge that is. Maybe somewhat tentatively, we offer that person up to our Lord, praying that He will return them to us in health. Then we hope we will not suffer loss.

God had promised Abraham that he would have descendants through Isaac. So when God asked Abraham to sacrifice Isaac, Abraham probably had trouble wrapping his brain around the idea. But the faithful man clung to the promise that he would have grandchildren by this son. Abraham even trusted that, should the Lord take Isaac's life, He could also resurrect the young man. Surely Abraham hoped that would not happen—and it didn't.

More important than the sacrifice of a son was the sacrifice of Abraham's heart. When nothing made sense, he still trusted God. No matter what, he knew God would provide a way out of this situation. And God did by providing the sacrificial ram.

God has ways out of our situations that we cannot even begin to imagine. When He asks us to make the heart sacrifice of trust in the face of the unknown, can we believe that a way out is available? When we make a sacrifice, we can do so in the clear knowledge that He has made the greatest sacrifice—His Son, Jesus.

FATHER GOD, NO SACRIFICE I CAN MAKE IS AS GREAT AS THE ONE YOU MADE IN YOUR SON, JESUS, WHO DIED FOR MY SINS. THANK YOU FOR TAKING CONTROL OF MY SIN PROBLEM AND BRINGING ME TO YOURSELF THROUGH HIM.

READY TO HELP

"For I have chosen you and will not throw you away.
Don't be afraid, for I am with you. Don't be discouraged,
for I am your God. I will strengthen you and help you.
I will hold you up with my victorious right hand. . . . For I
hold you by your right hand—I, the LORD your God.
And I say to you, 'Don't be afraid. I am here to help you.'"
ISAIAH 41:9–10, 13 NLT

Have you ever felt that you haven't been faithful to God and wondered if He's given up on you?

Israel hadn't been faithful. The nation had fallen into idolatry and ignored all God's warnings. The prophet Isaiah had done all he could to reach their hearts, but they'd shoved him—and God—away. If God were a human being, no one could have blamed Him for giving up on them.

But God is not like people. He had made a covenant with Israel, and despite the nation's weak faith, He could not become faithless. It's simply not in His nature.

That's not to say God approves of sin. He doesn't. But where we are frail or mistaken, He is not. Where we are faithless, He cannot be.

Though Israel had greatly wronged God, He would not

throw them away. For a time, most of the nation was transported to Babylon. Because no prophecies had gotten through to His people, He gave them a practical lesson in what it was like to live far from Him, under the thumb of a pagan tyrant. It was a picture of the results of sin.

But before they even left for Babylon, God encouraged His people. He would be with them and give them strength. They had nothing to fear. He who had made them His people would not desert them.

Have you failed God? He has never failed you. Turn to Him, and you will find Him at your side, ready to help. Confess and turn from sin, and you will be forgiven.

THANK YOU, LORD, FOR BEING SO FAITHFUL TO ME THAT EVEN SIN CANNOT DESTROY YOUR LOVE FOR ME. FORGIVE ME FOR MY SIN AND DRAW ME NEAR TO YOU AGAIN.

STILL IN CONTROL

But the word of God came to Shemaiah the man of God, saying, "Speak to Rehoboam the son of Solomon, king of Judah, and to all the house of Judah and Benjamin, and to the remnant of the people, saying, 'This is what the LORD says: "You shall not go up or fight against your brothers, the children of Israel. Return, every man to his house, for this thing is from Me."'" Therefore they listened to the word of the LORD and returned, according to the word of the LORD.
1 KINGS 12:22–24 SKJV

. . . .

Rehoboam inherited the throne of Israel from his father, Solomon. But the new king's harsh policies took advantage of his people and caused the northern part of the nation to rebel. Jeroboam became Israel's king, and Rehoboam was left ruling the tribes of Judah. The nation was split.

Though Rehoboam would have liked to jump into his chariot and call his men to arms, God gave him a message not to do so. This division was from the Lord.

Rehoboam treated his people badly, but he evidently didn't want to take on God. Obediently, he returned to Jerusalem.

Things did not go well for the northern kingdom, Israel, for Jeroboam led them into idolatry. And despite God's command to Rehoboam, peace did not exist between the two nations for the entirety of the two kings' lives (1 Kings 14:30).

We know how it is to watch a political system that's in trouble. Our leaders can be as unwise as Rehoboam was and as unfaithful to God, for Judah fell into idolatry too.

If we wish to have a perfect leader, we cannot look to humans. No man or woman can lead without error. No one has perfect wisdom and knowledge of what the future holds. For that we look to God. No matter how much our leaders fail, and even if they deny God altogether, God still has a plan for His people. We may struggle within a seemingly godless nation, yet the Lord blesses us and, through us, our nation.

LORD, NO MATTER HOW DISAPPOINTING OUR NATION'S LEADERSHIP IS, I TRUST THAT YOU ARE STILL IN CONTROL. MAY I BECOME A BLESSING TO MY COUNTRY BECAUSE I LOVE YOU.

PROVISION

*And He commanded the people to sit down on the ground,
and He took the seven loaves, and gave thanks and broke
them, and gave them to His disciples to set before them.
And they set them before the people. And they had a few small
fish. And He blessed them and also commanded them to be
set before them. So they ate and were filled, and they took up
seven baskets of the broken food that was left. And those who
had eaten were about four thousand. And He sent them away.*
MARK 8:6–9 SKJV

For three days, a multitude of people had followed Jesus
and listened to His teachings. As the time came for them to
leave, He felt compassion for them. How many would safely
reach home on empty stomachs? So He asked His doubting
disciples how much food was available. Their answer? Seven
loaves and a few small fish. A rather meager meal for four
thousand people.

But Jesus gave thanks for what God had provided and
blessed these bits. Then they were passed around to the crowd.
Amazingly, everyone ate their fill, and seven baskets of leftovers
were cleaned up at the end.

Without Jesus, the people would have trudged away with

growling stomachs, but when He put His hands on the food and gave the blessing, a miracle occurred. Emptiness became fullness. His listeners went home no doubt talking of the amazing feat that sped them safely on their way.

Sometimes, we feel emptiness in our lives, physically or spiritually. Maybe we'd like a bigger paycheck, or we may seek spiritual blessings that escape us. Remember that at least some of these people had gone days without food. Even those prepared with food probably didn't expect the teaching to go on that long. But their spirits drew them to remain with Jesus. And for that they were blessed.

If we remain with Jesus, though our provision seems a bit thin, in the end we, too, will be filled. The Spirit of Jesus fills our lives and makes provision for our real needs.

LORD, THANK YOU FOR PROVIDING FOR ME
PHYSICALLY AND SPIRITUALLY. WHEN PROVISION
SEEMS BARE, HELP ME TRUST IN YOU.

SWALLOWED UP?

Now the LORD had arranged for a great fish to swallow Jonah.
And Jonah was inside the fish for three days and three nights.
JONAH 1:17 NLT

The rebellious prophet Jonah refused God's mission to Nineveh. Not only was the mission dangerous, but how could Jonah bear to see salvation come to his nation's mortal enemies?

So Jonah boarded a ship to escape God's command. To get the attention of His runaway prophet, God had Jonah thrown overboard. Jonah 2:5–6 (NLT) describes that terrible experience: "I sank beneath the waves, and the waters closed over me. Seaweed wrapped itself around my head. I sank down to the very roots of the mountains. I was imprisoned in the earth, whose gates lock shut forever." The situation was dire. Clearly, God could have demanded the disobedient prophet's life. "But you, O LORD my God," Jonah continued, "snatched me from the jaws of death!" At death's door, Jonah remembered to pray, and God saved him by having him swallowed by a fish. That creature imprisoned Jonah for three days then spit him out on shore.

Finally, Jonah grudgingly obeyed God. He went to Nineveh, and his preaching was a great success. The Ninevites repented at the order of their king.

Yet Jonah took no joy in the success of his mission. He complained to God that he wanted to die.

More than 120,000 Ninevites were saved because God opened their hearts. Perhaps no one seemed less likely to respond to the Word of God than these violent people. Though God's power was shown, all Jonah could do was complain. That's where the biblical account ends.

Have you ever tried to escape from a plan God had for your life? How did that end? Logic should tell us that we can never escape His authority. But that's a good thing!

He who controls all creation oversees your life too. With Him, life will never swallow you up.

LORD, I DON'T WANT TO RESIST YOUR PLANS FOR MY LIFE. HELP ME TO WALK WHEREVER YOU LEAD.

SAFE!

The name of the Lord is a strong tower.
The righteous runs to it and is safe.
PROVERBS 18:10 SKJV

. . . .

Have you ever felt like running away from life? Maybe you're tired of the everyday burdens. Or maybe you just feel overwhelmed.

"Come to me, all of you who are weary and carry heavy burdens, and I will give you rest," Jesus promised (Matthew 11:28 NLT). There is no burden He cannot ease.

Just as a small child does not do well to run away from home, we adults do not improve our lives by running from God. Proverbs 18:10 tells us we need to run toward Him, not away. When we do that, we run into His strength.

"The name of the Lord" describes who He is and what He is like. Think of all the biblical descriptions of His nature, and remember that He is strong and powerful—and that He controls the lives of the righteous. This is what our God is like and what we can expect of Him. Running to Him is running to security.

As C. S. Lewis described the lion Aslan, his Christ figure in the Chronicles of Narnia, God "is not a tame lion." We cannot manipulate Him to follow our own plans and purposes. But

He is good. That is His perfect nature. All that comes from Him is also good.

We may fear the authority of earthly leaders and doubt their justice. But if we have accepted Jesus as Savior, we need not fear the power of God. He who makes us righteous also makes us safe. All we need to do is run to Him, our strong tower, when the world becomes dangerous and burdensome.

LORD, I THANK YOU THAT MY SAFETY LIES IN YOU. HELP ME TO RUN TO YOU WHEN THE WORLD SEEMS OVERWHELMING.

HIDDEN SIN

*"Israel has sinned, and they have also transgressed My
covenant that I commanded them. For they have even
taken of the accursed things. . . . Therefore the children
of Israel could not stand before their enemies. . .because
they were accursed. I will not be with you anymore,
unless you destroy the accursed from among you."*
JOSHUA 7:11–12 SKJV

Before Joshua and his warriors attacked the city of Jericho, God warned them that everything in the city belonged to Him and should be destroyed.

But one man, fueled by greed, disobeyed this command. Achan stole a beautiful cloak, silver, and gold and hid them inside his tent.

For a while, Achan seemed to get away with his sin. But when the warriors attacked the small community of Ai, they lost this battle that should have been a breeze to win. That's when God made it clear that one man's disobedience had affected an entire nation.

One by one, Joshua had each tribe, clan, and household brought before him until it was clear that Achan's was the offending household. Confronted about his sin, the man admitted to it. Achan and his family and all their animals were stoned in the Valley of Achor. Then they were burned, just as Jericho had been.

This punishment may seem drastic, but it pictures how seriously God takes sin. He made a holy covenant with His people. Achan disobeyed God's clear prohibition and paid a terrible price for the whole nation to see.

God takes the holiness of His people seriously, and He knows all their hidden sins. Truly the sins of one person *can* damage a whole nation. To avoid the destruction of His people, God had to nip sin in the bud.

When we sin, we also break the covenant of God. Yet in His mercy, He offers us forgiveness through the sacrifice of Jesus. Will we take seriously the call to turn from sin, or like Achan, will we try to hide it in our tents?

LORD, I DO NOT WANT TO HARM MY FAMILY AND EVEN MY NATION WITH SIN. SHOW ME WHERE I NEED TO OBEY YOU, AND MAKE ME FAITHFUL TO YOUR WORD.

VICTORIOUS REBELS

And the Rab-shakeh said to them, "Say now to Hezekiah,
'This is what the great king, the king of Assyria, says: "What
confidence is this in which you trust? You say (but they are
only empty words), 'I have a plan and strength for war.'
Now on whom do you trust, that you rebel against me?"'"
2 KINGS 18:19–20 SKJV

In the sixth year of King Hezekiah's reign, Judah had seen its sister state, the northern kingdom of Israel, conquered by the warlike Assyrians, who then shipped the people of Israel to their land.

Now, in Hezekiah's fourteenth year as king, King Sennacherib of Assyria set his sights on Judah. He captured the fortified cities and headed for Jerusalem. There, the field officer (or Rab-shakeh) spoke with Hezekiah's officials, belittling their strength. Then he tried to cause division in the Jews by belittling God and reminding them that Hezekiah had taken down the high places of pagan worship (2 Kings 18:22). Their God, he intimated, would be of no help.

Hezekiah, who was faithful to God, put on sackcloth and prayed. Perhaps he was reminded of God's promise to be His people's military leader if they remained faithful to Him (Deuteronomy 7:12–13, 21–24).

Assyria had the biggest and best army of the day. Things looked grim for Hezekiah, who had rebelled against this superpower. But Hezekiah's God was not simply a wooden idol. Removing the high places of worship did not influence His power at all.

No superpower can beat God. No weapons of war or crafty military leaders can ultimately defy Him. It was true then, and it's true today. And best of all, if you are on His side, you too cannot lose. Those who rebel against sin and commit to the ways of God will never fail to be defended by Him.

THANK YOU, LORD, FOR BEING VICTORIOUS OVER EVERY ENEMY I WILL EVER FACE. I PLACE MY LIFE IN YOUR HANDS AND COMMIT TO OBEYING YOU.

A STUNNING STORY

And it came to pass that night that the angel of the LORD went out and struck one hundred and eighty-five thousand in the camp of the Assyrians, and when they arose early in the morning, behold, they were all dead corpses. So Sennacherib, king of Assyria, departed and went away and returned and remained in Nineveh.

2 KINGS 19:35–36 SKJV

In one of the most stunning Bible stories, God proved His power and protected His people as He kept the Assyrian army from attacking the holy city of Jerusalem. Just when the Assyrian army was camped before His city, God stepped in to show who He is—and how powerful.

The pagan King Sennacherib had threatened Judah's King Hezekiah, but then became distracted by other battles. So Sennacherib sent a message to Hezekiah that said, "Do not let your God in whom you trust deceive you, saying, 'Jerusalem shall not be delivered into the hand of the king of Assyria'" (2 Kings 19:10 SKJV). The Assyrian planned on coming back to finish the business he had with Jerusalem.

Hezekiah got the message, brought the letter before God in His temple, and prayed powerfully for God's help against

Judah's enemies. But he hardly could have imagined the solution God had for his problem. When the Jewish king went to bed, a live army sat at the gates of his city. Early in the morning, not one man walked the camp outside Jerusalem. Every single Assyrian was dead.

King Sennacherib heard a threatening rumor and headed for his own country. There, as Isaiah had prophesied, two of his sons killed him while he was worshiping his pagan god (2 Kings 19:6–7, 36–37).

Assyria's blasphemy of God proved to be a lie. God's protection of His people occurred in a most memorable way. Who can forget this story of God's power in the face of blasphemy?

God may very well be writing a stunning story in your life. Are you just waiting to see what He has in store for you?

LORD, I WANT YOU TO WRITE A STUNNING STORY
IN MY LIFE TODAY. MAY THOSE WHO DON'T BELIEVE
SEE A TESTIMONY TO YOU IN ALL I DO.

NO DICTATOR

"Return and tell Hezekiah the leader of My people,
'This is what the LORD, the God of David your father
says: "I have heard your prayer. I have seen your tears.
Behold, I will heal you. On the third day you shall go up
to the house of the LORD. And I will add fifteen years to
your days, and I will deliver you and this city from the
hand of the king of Assyria, and I will defend this city
for My own sake and for My servant David's sake."'"
2 KINGS 20:5–6 SKJV

The prophet Isaiah came to King Hezekiah of Judah with bad news. Isaiah told the king that God was ordering him to prepare for death. The godly Hezekiah—of whom 2 Kings 18:6 (SKJV) says, "He clung to the LORD and did not depart from following Him but observed His commandments, which the LORD commanded Moses"—had just seen God destroy the Assyrian army of 185,000 men. In prayer the king reminded God of his faithfulness, and the verses above were the Lord's response. Generously, God added fifteen years to the king's life and defended and delivered Jerusalem.

God was in control. And He blessed Hezekiah with more years to his life and peace for his land. The faithful king did not bludgeon his Lord into providing these blessings. He simply asked in faith.

We, too, serve this all-powerful God, and we can ask Him for whatever we need. . .even for things we want. God may be powerful, but He is no dictator. We interact with Him; that's the way He wants our relationship to be. Yet He has the final say about everything because He has a long view of our lives and our world. He knows if giving us fifteen more years of life—or whatever else we ask for—will be a curse or a blessing. Knowing that, we can submit thankfully to His will.

LORD, THANK YOU FOR WANTING AN INTERACTIVE
RELATIONSHIP WITH ME. I'M GRATEFUL YOU
KNOW WHAT IS BEST IN MY LIFE. HELP ME
TRUST IN YOU, EVEN WHEN YOU SAY NO.

HANGING ON

Then Satan answered the LORD and said, "Does Job fear God
for nothing? Have You not made a hedge around him and
around his house and around all that he has on every side?
You have blessed the work of his hands, and his possessions
have increased in the land. But put forth Your hand now and
touch all that he has, and he will curse You to Your face."
JOB 1:9–11 SKJV

One day when the angels presented themselves to the Lord, Satan came along too. God bragged about His servant Job, who was blameless and upright. Jealous Satan objected that Job served God only because He perfectly protected Job. "Take away Your protection, and You'll see a different side of Job," the evil one suggested.

God must have had a lot of faith in Job. He allowed Satan to touch all that Job owned, including his family members. But Satan could not touch Job himself.

Though he lost nearly all he owned, Job responded, "Naked I came out of my mother's womb and naked I shall return there. The LORD gave and the LORD has taken away. Blessed be the name of the LORD" (Job 1:21 SKJV). Then scripture reports, "In all this Job did not sin or charge God foolishly" (verse 22 SKJV).

Still jealous, Satan returned and told God that if he could physically afflict poor Job, the man would lose his faith.

So God allowed Satan to harm Job, though not to the point of death. Confused, confronted by friends who insisted he'd sinned, and told by his wife that he should curse God and die, Job never lost faith. As he hung on doggedly amid nearly unbearable trials, Job knew that God was still somehow in the middle of this. He would not give up on the Lord he loved. And in the end, Job's trials proved the making of his faith. He learned what God was really like and experienced His approval.

When we face trials, God isn't trying to ruin us. Perhaps we are becoming a testimony of faith. If we hold on, His approval may soon become apparent.

LORD, HELP ME TO HOLD ON DURING
TRIALS AND KEEP MY FAITH IN YOU.

IN GOD'S HANDS

I want to know Christ and experience the mighty power
that raised him from the dead. I want to suffer with
him, sharing in his death, so that one way or another
I will experience the resurrection from the dead!
PHILIPPIANS 3:10–11 NLT

It's easy to see that we lack God's immense power. Yet His Spirit puts His power to work in our lives, and God's power lives through us! Of course, we never control His power. But the more we connect with Him and seek to do His will, the more God's Spirit becomes active in our lives.

And we need this power if we have any hope of achieving righteousness. The apostle Paul—a passionate, highly educated Jewish leader converted by the personal intervention of Jesus Himself—learned that he was powerless to make himself good. Ultimately, he learned and wrote that "the righteous will live by faith" (Romans 1:17 NIV).

Pursuing God's love and favor through our own strength is a dead end. We simply can't rely on ourselves.

As he pressed on in his faith—suffering mightily for it—Paul wanted to experience the power that raised Jesus from death. The apostle counted nothing he'd lost by following Jesus as more important than all he gained in Christ. He did not even fear death, because that would just lead to his resurrection. The power of God will raise us with Jesus (2 Corinthians 4:14).

Most of us are in no rush to experience death. But we know that even through death, God is in control. We need not fear, because Jesus conquered death, and that experience leads finally to the believer's resurrection.

Even beyond our last breath, God remains in charge of our lives. Our job is simply to trust Him.

THANK YOU, LORD JESUS, FOR CONQUERING DEATH
FOR ME. IN ALL THINGS I AM IN YOUR HANDS.

FINDING PEACE

*"Do not suppose that I have come to bring peace
to the earth. I did not come to bring peace, but a
sword. . . . Whoever finds their life will lose it, and
whoever loses their life for my sake will find it."*

MATTHEW 10:34, 39 NIV

We tend to believe that knowing God means we will experience a peaceful life. That can be true, because through Jesus we have spiritual peace with our Lord. When we are in the center of God's will, we experience peace.

But we live in a world that largely does not acknowledge the authority of God. We cannot separate ourselves from our unbelieving world, and sometimes we must stand against wrongdoing. Even in faithful churches, disagreements can lead to disturbance. Sometimes good, well-meaning people end up amid dissension, and finding peace again can be a challenge.

We also can experience spiritual war within ourselves if we try to resist the truths of God's Word. Then the double-edged sword of God's Word may cut up our internal peace because our attitudes slipped away from His will.

If our lives seem out of our control, let's admit that we never really were in charge—at least not completely. God allows us to direct our lives in many ways. He gives us freedom to choose good and the ability to avoid evil, yet our sin-sick hearts don't live completely in His will. Try as we might, daily we find ourselves coming to Him for forgiveness. And that is God's solution for the restless soul. As we put our lives in line with His will, we find healing.

Are you feeling restless? It does not mean God has lost control. You may just be sensing a lack of peace reflecting the world around you. Or it may mean you reached out and tried to grab the reins of your life. Whatever the case, God has things well in hand. Go to Him, seeking His will and way. . .and peace.

LORD, I WANT TO LIVE IN PEACE WITH YOU,
NO MATTER WHAT DISTURBANCES SURROUND ME.

CHURCH AND STATE

*But truly I am full of power by the Spirit of the LORD,
and of judgment and of might, to declare to Jacob his
transgression and to Israel his sin. Hear this, I ask you, you
heads of the house of Jacob and princes of the house of Israel,
who hate judgment and pervert all equity. They build up
Zion with blood and Jerusalem with iniquity. Their heads
judge for reward, their priests teach for wages, and their
prophets divine for money. Yet they will lean on the LORD
and say, "Is the LORD not among us? No evil can come
upon us." Therefore, because of you, Zion shall be plowed
like a field. And Jerusalem shall become heaps, and the
mountain of the house like the high places of the forest.*
MICAH 3:8–12 SKJV

Have dishonest leaders, whether they are in the church or in political groups, read and believed the minor prophets? If so, they should repent and do so quickly. For just as God judged Israel and Jacob, bringing their enemies down on them and destroying their countries, He has the power to remove today's crooked politicians and bent church leaders from office.

Relying on a false claim to God's favor will not save the dishonest and selfish. No one can avoid evil with untrue claims of faith. Those who truly believe show it by their actions and lifestyles, which will accord with God's will.

When we put people into office, we need to look at their lifestyles and vote accordingly. If we want our country to flourish, we need to bring our faith to the table at voting time. Because we want our churches to do well, we need to support the people who show real faith in action. Otherwise, our churches and government will "become heaps."

Most of all, we need to pray for God to establish good, moral leaders who will do His will. Then God's power can be shown in church and state, and we will see His control at work.

LORD, REMIND ME TO PRAY REGULARLY FOR
LEADERS OF CHURCH AND STATE. I WOULD SEE
THE BLESSINGS OF YOUR POWER THROUGH
PEOPLE WHO KNOW, LOVE, AND SERVE YOU.

A CRITICAL SPIRIT?

One Sabbath Jesus was going through the grainfields,
and his disciples began to pick some heads of grain, rub them
in their hands and eat the kernels. Some of the Pharisees asked,
"Why are you doing what is unlawful on the Sabbath?"
LUKE 6:1–2 NIV

Nowhere in the law did God say that hungry travelers could not pick grain; in fact, Deuteronomy 23:25 says it is okay for hungry people to gather a small amount of it. But the Pharisees had added so many rules to scripture's commands that they took Jesus to task because His disciples picked grain on the Sabbath. To them, their own backbreaking rules were as important as scripture.

Jesus reminded them of David's hungry men who had eaten the bread of the presence when David was fleeing from Saul. Ahimelech the priest was willing to give holy bread to David and his men as long as they were living purely.

Then Jesus told His critics that He was Lord of the Sabbath (Luke 6:5). (And surely, being God, He knew what should or should not be done on the Sabbath.)

Sometimes, God is not such a nitpicker as we can be. He never punished David and his hungry men for taking holy bread, and the disciples received no punishment for taking enough to fill their stomachs on a Sabbath day. God knew their hearts and understood the disciples were not working—which would have been banned on the day of rest.

Jesus is Lord of the Sabbath because He is God. He understands our hearts and all that God requires of us in His Word. He doesn't give awards for nitpicking on minor issues. Let's remember that when we look at another Christian's actions or beliefs and start feeling critical. God is in control of that believer's life and ours, and maybe He's asking us to show compassion instead of criticism.

LORD, I WANT TO OBEY YOUR WORD, AND I WANT TO HELP OTHERS DO SO TOO. BUT DON'T LET ME FALL INTO A CRITICAL SPIRIT THAT DOES NOT GLORIFY YOU. I WANT YOU TO BE IN CONTROL OF EVERY PART OF MY LIFE.

TRUTH INDEED

"This is what the LORD says—your Redeemer, who formed you in the womb: I am the LORD, the Maker of all things, who stretches out the heavens, who spreads out the earth by myself, who foils the signs of false prophets and makes fools of diviners, who overthrows the learning of the wise and turns it into nonsense."

ISAIAH 44:24–25 NIV

The Lord God, your Redeemer and Creator, defines truth and rules over it. When spiritual leaders speak falsehood, He knows and proves it. When unbelievers come up with ludicrous ideas, He shows that it is nonsense. Though it may take a while for truth to come out, be sure that it will. For God, not people, created and controls truth.

Looking for the source of truth? God proclaimed through the prophet Isaiah, "I, the LORD, speak the truth; I declare what is right" (Isaiah 45:19 NIV). We need not look all over the world. No hidden, foreign wisdom exists that we must ferret out. God's Word shows us His ultimate truth.

Even seemingly wise people of this world become foolish as they stand before God's wisdom. For the Creator knows infinitely more than any human. Scientists and philosophers perform experiments and study endlessly, but they will never have the wisdom of God unless they seek it. Even then, no one can comprehend more than a small portion of God's wisdom. What sinful human can comprehend all that a holy God is and does?

Yet as we seek to know truth, Jesus gave us the direction we must head in, declaring, "I am the way and the truth and the life" (John 14:6 NIV). We find His truth when we know and live in Him. The psalmist wrote, "LORD, who may dwell in your sacred tent? Who may live on your holy mountain? The one whose walk is blameless, who does what is righteous, who speaks the truth from their heart" (Psalm 15:1–2 NIV). On our own, we can never become blameless, righteous speakers of truth. Only by knowing and living in Jesus do we find the truth indeed.

LORD, MY LIVING IN YOUR TRUTH SHOWS YOUR
CONTROL OVER MY LIFE. HELP MY ACTIONS TO
DEMONSTRATE YOUR WORK IN MY LIFE

ENDING INJUSTICE

*How long, LORD, must I call for help, but you do not
listen? Or cry out to you, "Violence!" but you do not
save? Why do you make me look at injustice? Why do
you tolerate wrongdoing? Destruction and violence are
before me; there is strife, and conflict abounds.*

HABAKKUK 1:2–3 NIV

· ·

How often do we see injustices and wonder what God is thinking? How can He allow such things to go on? *Does He know
and care?* we may wonder.

Certainly God does. He knew and cared in Habakkuk's day,
and He has not changed. Yet after Habakkuk cried out to God,
he was probably surprised by God's answer: "I am raising up
the Babylonians," God responded, "that ruthless and impetuous
people, who sweep across the whole earth to seize dwellings not
their own" (Habakkuk 1:6 NIV).

Habakkuk probably hoped to hear that the people he
preached to were going to turn and have faith in the Lord,
that his ministry was not in vain. Though the prophet was
weary of their lack of response to God's message, an attack by
his people's enemies scarcely fit Habakkuk's expectations. But
he immediately knew why God was doing this: "You, LORD,

have appointed them to execute judgment; you, my Rock, have ordained them to punish. Your eyes are too pure to look on evil; you cannot tolerate wrongdoing" (Habakkuk 1:12–13 NIV).

God is very patient with sinners. He does not rush to give us the punishment we certainly deserve; He offers each sinner an opportunity to repent. But that doesn't mean any of us have an endless timeline.

Expecting God, who controls all things, to put up with disobedience forever is to think He's a wimp—and He certainly isn't that. Nonbelievers often condemn God because bad things happen: "A good God would never allow such and such to happen." In doing so, they create their own god, not the one of scripture. Their god will never be just and in control.

Wrongdoing won't last forever. God's ultimate judgment will make all things right.

THANK YOU, LORD, FOR YOUR COMPASSION
IN JUDGMENT. YET I KNOW THAT YOU WILL
EVENTUALLY MAKE ALL THINGS RIGHT.

PROTECTING HIS PEOPLE

And when Haman saw that Mordecai did not bow or show him reverence, then Haman was full of anger. And he disdained to lay hands on Mordecai alone, for they had revealed to him the people of Mordecai. For that reason Haman sought to destroy all the Jews—the people of Mordecai—who were throughout the whole kingdom of Ahasuerus.
ESTHER 3:5–6 SKJV

Haman was a dangerous man, filled with pride and hatred. Mordecai refused to bow down to him. His reasons aren't specifically stated in scripture. But because of Mordecai's decision, Haman considered him an enemy and plotted to destroy him. To cover his tracks, Haman decided to kill all of Mordecai's people too. Haman had learned that Mordecai was Jewish.

Though Haman had information Mordecai wanted to keep quiet, even that did not give him the advantage that he thought he had. All the intelligence gathering in the world cannot take God's control away from Him. God loves and protects His people.

Did Haman miss out on the fact that the queen was Mordecai's cousin? While she was inviting him to banquets, did this government official really think she was honoring him more than Mordecai? If so, he was completely wrong. Esther was God's silent weapon against His people's enemies. He had placed her in just the right place at just the right time. And He gave her the ability to stand for the Jews even though she risked her own life.

Does some danger seem to threaten you? God is still in control of your life. Be alert to His leading, and He will protect you as one of His people.

THANK YOU FOR PROTECTING ME FROM THE
HATRED OF OTHERS, LORD. LET NO OTHER
PERSON'S ATTITUDE HARM MY FAITH IN YOU.

NO BULLYING

"And then the sign of the Son of Man shall appear in heaven,
and then all the tribes of the earth shall mourn, and they shall
see the Son of Man coming in the clouds of heaven with power
and great glory. And He shall send His angels with a great
sound of a trumpet, and they shall gather together His elect
from the four winds, from one end of heaven to the other."
MATTHEW 24:30–31 SKJV

Jesus foretold a day when He will suddenly appear again on earth. For some it will be a wonderful day when they will be gathered into His kingdom. But in all the tribes of the earth there will be mourning by those who haven't accepted Jesus as Savior.

As we hear all the worldly criticisms of God, we can remember that we have yet to see the end of the story. While unbelievers critique the way God does things, let's keep in mind that Jesus first came as a sacrifice to save us from our sins. He who was meek and lowly (Matthew 11:29) will one day come in all His power, showing His great glory.

On that day His critics will have a change of heart. No longer will they deny His power; instead, they will grieve their lost opportunity. Judgment will stand before them, and the one they once denied and denigrated will be their judge.

The fact that God has yet to deal with every wrong doesn't indicate He will never set things right. The fact that He never strong-arms people into faith doesn't indicate He lacks power. Those who ignore or deny Him have made a choice and will account for their decision.

Strength does not require bullying, and God never hustles anyone into His kingdom. Faith is a choice, and God woos people. Being clasped by His strong arms is a joy, not a harsh demand.

But those who reject His wooing must mourn the loss of the bridegroom.

LORD, THANK YOU FOR YOUR GENTLE TOUCH
IN DRAWING ME INTO YOUR KINGDOM.
I CANNOT WAIT FOR YOU TO COME IN GLORY.

DON'T WORRY

"No one can serve two masters. Either you will hate the one and love the other, or you will be devoted to the one and despise the other. You cannot serve both God and money. Therefore I tell you, do not worry about your life, what you will eat or drink; or about your body, what you will wear. Is not life more than food, and the body more than clothes?"

MATTHEW 6:24–25 NIV

How much time do we spend thinking about money, worrying about money, wondering if we will have enough money?

Are we serving gold rather than God?

Of course we need money, and we should use what God gives us wisely. But how many dollars we have in the bank or invested in the stock market doesn't indicate whether we have a good spiritual life. How much we love God and trust Him for our provision does.

How many Christians will find, in eternity, that their use of money was their biggest weakness? How many people of limited means are happier and more faithful than those with large homes and portfolios?

God directly tells us we cannot serve Him and money at the same time. When we worry about money, we are not trusting the God who promised to care for us. We try to take control of the future because we fear that someday we will not have enough for even the basics of life.

Jesus went on to remind us that God cares for the birds and flowers. How could He fail to care for His people? Times of real financial need may be moments when we see how faithfully God provides for us. As we offer up our needs to Him, we see the care He has for our entire lives. Fickle money never provides for us as well as God does.

LORD, I WANT TO SERVE YOU, NOT ANY FORM
OF MONEY. HELP ME TO TRUST THAT YOU ARE
ALWAYS IN CONTROL OF ALL MY NEEDS.

JESUS' AUTHORITY

The centurion replied, "Lord, I do not deserve to have you come under my roof. But just say the word, and my servant will be healed. For I myself am a man under authority, with soldiers under me. I tell this one, 'Go,' and he goes; and that one, 'Come,' and he comes. I say to my servant, 'Do this,' and he does it." When Jesus heard this, he was amazed and said to those following him, "Truly I tell you, I have not found anyone in Israel with such great faith."

MATTHEW 8:8–10 NIV

The Roman centurion who asked Jesus to heal his servant must have thought seriously on his way to meet the Master. For when Jesus offered to heal his servant, the soldier—aware that entry into a Gentile home would make Jesus ritually unclean—offered another solution: "Just say the word, Jesus, and I know it will be done." The soldier recognized the authority of Jesus over any illness, even the paralysis that afflicted his valued servant.

Such trust amazed Jesus. He might have expected it of a Jew, but a Roman—who certainly had a limited knowledge of the true God, even if he had come to faith in Him—was showing greater faith than people who had grown up knowing God's commands and living in the security that they were His people.

Even today, the centurion's faith amazes us. He was willing to throw his hopes for someone he cared about onto Jesus' shoulders and trusted that healing would come from it.

When someone we love is sick, can we give that person over to Jesus' authority? Though we trust in Him, we know that not everyone who prays sees complete healing.

But who else do we have to hope in? Where will unbelief land us? How much better it is to accept the authority of Jesus and trust in Him!

LORD, YOU HAVE AUTHORITY OVER EVERY ILLNESS, AND YOU CAN HEAL WHEN HUMAN ABILITIES ARE USELESS. NO MATTER WHAT ILLS I OR MY FAMILY EXPERIENCE, I PLACE MY TRUST IN YOU.

INFIRMITY-FREE

*When the evening had come, they brought to Him
many who were possessed with demons. And He cast out the
spirits with His word and healed all who were sick, that what
was spoken by Isaiah the prophet might be fulfilled, saying:
"He Himself took our infirmities and bore our sicknesses."*
MATTHEW 8:16–17 SKJV

Our spirits are deeply connected with our bodies. When one hurts, the other can feel pain too. When Jesus healed people during His time on earth, He kept the whole person in mind. Where sin had given Satan entrance into a life, He cast out the demons that influenced the person and healed the broken body.

Still today, illnesses may be limited by His hand. If we experience physical suffering, Jesus still provides healing and support in our trials.

We'd like to think that every infirmity could leave our bodies and spirits in a moment. It would be wonderful to be totally whole, body and spirit. We may be disappointed to learn that some sin still dogs our steps and other illnesses plague us. Has God failed us? Has He lost His power? Hardly.

"The last enemy that shall be destroyed is death," the apostle Paul warned us (1 Corinthians 15:26 SKJV). As the firstfruits of the dead (verse 20), Jesus gives us hope for complete healing, even though we have not yet seen it. When God heals us all, body and soul, death will no longer have a place or power over humanity. Without illness, death cannot afflict us.

Today, we experience the work Christ *has* done on our infirmities and sicknesses. Though sin has not totally lost all its power over us, we see His work in our lives and a lessening of sin's influence. Though we may not lose every impact of sin, we rejoice at the victories faith in Jesus gives us.

And one day, the last enemy will be destroyed. We will be raised with Christ and live eternally. As John Donne declared, "Death, thou shalt die!"

LORD, I LOOK FORWARD TO THE DAY WHEN
SPIRITUAL AND PHYSICAL INFIRMITIES ARE GONE
PERMANENTLY. THANK YOU FOR THE PROMISE
THAT ONE DAY I WILL BE COMPLETELY FREED.

OUR REFUGE

The nations raged; the kingdoms were moved.
He uttered His voice; the earth melted. The LORD of
hosts is with us; the God of Jacob is our refuge.
PSALM 46:6–7 SKJV

No matter the disaster that lies before us—storms or earthquakes or the wars caused by human disagreements—we need not fear. God is still in control and always has been. Nothing lies beyond His authority. "Wars and rumors of wars" (Matthew 24:6 NIV) may tempt us to fear, yet God calls us to remain faithful; we will always have refuge in Him.

While the world seems to be hurtling toward disaster, the God who can melt the earth or end the storm still manages everything. As Lord of hosts, He is the supreme commander. Even better, He is with us, not half a world away or in another kingdom. He is our refuge, the nearby strong tower we run to (Proverbs 18:10).

And just think: even in the worst situations, how could God lose track of the ones for whom His Son died?

Do you ever feel that life is out of control? Then remind yourself of God's nature. Not only is He powerful, and able to melt the earth—He is also merciful and loving. When we fear, He calls on us to find refuge in Him. And He never fails.

Should we find ourselves in the middle of a storm, He will protect and provide for us. Because of the storm, we may see Him care for us in amazing ways that stir our faith even more than we'd expect.

Though nations rage, our hearts lie at peace in our Lord. He is our true refuge.

LORD, I THANK YOU FOR BEING MY REFUGE,
WHETHER THE EARTH SHAKES BENEATH MY FEET OR
WAR SEEMS IMMINENT. I AM GLAD I CAN RELY ON YOU
IN THE WORST CIRCUMSTANCES. HELP ME TO TRUST
IN YOU NO MATTER WHAT HAPPENS AROUND ME.

CERTAIN RETURN

"This vision is for a future time. It describes the end, and it will be fulfilled. If it seems slow in coming, wait patiently, for it will surely take place. It will not be delayed."

<small>HABAKKUK 2:3 NLT</small>

Habakkuk saw the downward path his people were taking as they walked away from God. *Why is God waiting?* he wondered. Justice seemed to be denied in the law courts. Violence and arguments surrounded Habakkuk. Would the Lord allow this to continue?

Then God told the prophet He'd give the Babylonians power over His people. That didn't seem like a solution. Though God's people had gone astray, surely they were better than those pagans from Babylon. How could a holy God allow this to happen? Would He have His people destroyed?

God told the prophet that he'd foreseen a future downfall of the Jewish people. They might have turned back their punishment by seeking forgiveness, but of course they didn't. Stuck in their sins, they determinedly kept heading for destruction.

God warned Habakkuk that while His people waited, they should not assume God had changed His mind. The prophecy would happen, even if it was slow in coming.

Faithful Christians are in a similar situation concerning the second coming of Christ. Matthew 24 describes this event and the false prophets who will attempt to confuse people before Jesus returns and the world is judged.

Knowing that the Lord will come, we can wait patiently and faithfully, obeying His Word and calling others to believe in Him. What we cannot do is give up or deny His prophecy. Though we have yet to see it fulfilled, God has spoken—and no earthly power will change His plan. Nothing hastens, changes, or delays His intentions. Just as God sent Babylon against His nation, He will send His Son at the right moment.

Will you be ready for His return?

LORD, I WANT TO BE FAITHFUL WHILE I WAIT FOR YOUR RETURN AND JUDGMENT. THANK YOU FOR WARNING US. MAY I BE PREPARED FOR YOUR CERTAIN APPEARANCE.

PERFECT BENEFITS

And as [Saul] journeyed, he came near Damascus, and suddenly a light from heaven shone all around him. And he fell to the earth and heard a voice saying to him, "Saul, Saul, why are you persecuting Me?" And he said, "Who are You, Lord?" And the Lord said, "I am Jesus, whom you are persecuting. It is hard for you to kick against the barbs." And trembling and astonished, he said, "Lord, what do You want me to do?" And the Lord said to him, "Arise, and go into the city, and you shall be told what you must do."
ACTS 9:3–6 SKJV

. . . .

Though he sought to be faithful to God, Saul went about it the wrong way. When he saw what Christians were doing to his faith, he set out to correct their "mistakes." Not only did he approve of Stephen's stoning, he also personally dragged off Christians and saw them committed to prison (Acts 8:1–3).

Many Christians escaped persecution and scattered across the Mediterranean world. With them came the gospel message— not exactly the outcome this dedicated Pharisee had in mind.

What Saul didn't have in mind was part of the perfect plan of God. Without this persecution, Christians might have been slower to reach the world. What's more, God had an even larger plan in mind: Jesus met Saul on the road to Damascus, converted the former persecutor, and turned him into an apostle. Once his blindness was healed, Saul immediately began spreading the gospel.

No Christian could have imagined the outcome of Saul's persecution. Those languishing in jail could never have foreseen its benefits. Indeed, without Saul—who became known by the Roman name Paul—the gospel might never have spread as far west as Spain.

When we don't see benefits of our faithfulness, we need to rely on God's greater plan. What we don't know, He sees perfectly.

LORD, SOMETIMES MY LIFE MAKES LITTLE
SENSE, BUT I KNOW YOU HAVE A PLAN IN MIND.
HELP ME TO TRUST IN YOU ALWAYS.

PROMISES KEPT

Scripture foresaw that God would justify the Gentiles by faith, and announced the gospel in advance to Abraham: "All nations will be blessed through you."

<small>GALATIANS 3:8 NIV</small>

After Abraham was willing to sacrifice his son Isaac, God promised, "I will surely bless you and make your descendants as numerous as the stars in the sky and as the sand on the seashore. Your descendants will take possession of the cities of their enemies, and through your offspring all nations on earth will be blessed, because you have obeyed me" (Genesis 22:17–18 NIV).

We may wonder if God's promises to Abraham have come true. After all, the Jews have had a challenging history.

They gained the Promised Land under Joshua and lost it again, due to their own faithlessness to God. After being dragged from their land by the Assyrians and Babylonians, they saw God return them to it again. Following their rejection of Jesus as Messiah, the Jews were dispersed to all the nations, yet He brought them again into one nation, as He promised. Isaiah 66:8 (NIV)—"Who has ever heard of such things? Who has ever seen things like this? Can a country be born in a day or a nation be brought forth in a moment? Yet no sooner is Zion in labor than she gives birth to her children"—was fulfilled for a second time after World War II when the United Nations voted to establish a Jewish homeland.

God is not finished with His promises. One day, the nation of Israel will recognize Jesus as Messiah, and He will win the victory over all nations (Zechariah 12:10; Psalm 2:6–9; Revelation 11:15).

In the meantime, the whole world has been blessed through Jesus, the fulfillment of the Abrahamic covenant.

God keeps His promises. Are you having a challenging time in your life? Trust in the promises God has given you. He is always in full control.

LORD, THANK YOU FOR KEEPING YOUR PROMISES.
I TRUST YOU WILL KEEP THEM IN MY LIFE TOO.

IN CONTROL

"God is not human, that he should lie, not a human being, that he should change his mind. Does he speak and then not act? Does he promise and not fulfill? I have received a command to bless; he has blessed, and I cannot change it."

NUMBERS 23:19–20 NIV

King Balak of Moab saw the invading Israelites heading for his kingdom and feared them. So he called on Balaam, a well-known diviner and prophet, to curse the attackers.

Balaam is a bit confusing to many Christians. Was he really a prophet? Did he know God? Why was he trying to change God's mind about the Israelites? In the Old Testament, Balaam is referred to as one who practiced divination (Joshua 13:22), which God had forbidden (Deuteronomy 18:14), and as the one who tempted the Jews at Peor (Numbers 31:16). The New Testament repeatedly speaks negatively of him (2 Peter 2:15; Jude 11; Revelation 2:14).

So it's surprising that Balaam eventually got God's message right. God had to use a donkey to get the point across—namely, that the polytheistic prophet should say only what the Lord said, not anything that would please the king. Balaam tried hard to get God to agree with the king, but He who is faithful would not change His mind. God finally convinced Balaam that all the gold and silver of Moab couldn't purchase a curse against Israel.

Eventually, even the king of Moab understood that Balaam had no authority over God's decisions. So he looked for a compromise: "Neither curse them at all nor bless them at all!" (Numbers 23:25 NIV). Doubtless fearful for his own life, the prophet admitted he could do nothing but bless.

Though our enemies may seek to bring ill on God's people, nothing is ever done outside the realm of His will. No one can touch us without His allowing it. Whatever happens, He is always in control.

LORD, THANK YOU THAT NOTHING CAN BE DONE TO ME THAT YOU ARE UNAWARE OF. MAY I NEVER FORGET THE MANY BLESSINGS I'VE ALREADY RECEIVED FROM YOU.

GOD'S VICTORY

Gideon and the hundred men with him reached the edge
of the camp at the beginning of the middle watch, just after
they had changed the guard. They blew their trumpets and
broke the jars that were in their hands. The three companies
blew the trumpets and smashed the jars. Grasping the torches in
their left hands and holding in their right hands the trumpets
they were to blow, they shouted, "A sword for the LORD and
for Gideon!" While each man held his position around the
camp, all the Midianites ran, crying out as they fled.

JUDGES 7:19–21 NIV

Gideon, the weakest man in the weakest clan of Israel,
brought together some of the Israelites to fight the powerful
Midianites. Midian's army had threatened Israel by coming to
the Valley of Jezreel. So Gideon and his warriors gathered at
the spring of Harod.

There God allowed all the men who trembled with fear
to leave the army. Twenty-two thousand exited. Now Gideon
faced the enemy with an army of ten thousand. But to God's
mind, that was still too many men. He knew that if a large army
won, the nation would become proud and claim the victory as
their own. So God continued to whittle down their numbers

according to the way they drank water. Those who lapped like a dog were chosen—just three hundred men.

When He called Gideon to save his nation, God had promised to be with him. The men went into battle armed with trumpets, and torches in jars. They blew the trumpets, smashed open the jars, and cried out, "A sword for the LORD and for Gideon!"

Their enemy fled.

God was certainly in control of a battle won by three hundred men. Likewise, even if we feel too weak to serve God, His Spirit can empower us to do much for Him. Then He shines brightly before all who see our success.

LORD, I'M THRILLED AT THE WAY YOU USE
ME FOR THE GOOD OF YOUR KINGDOM,
DESPITE MY WEAKNESSES. THANK YOU.

DON'T FEAR

*About three o'clock in the morning Jesus came toward
them, walking on the water. When the disciples saw
him walking on the water, they were terrified. In their
fear, they cried out, "It's a ghost!" But Jesus spoke to
them at once. "Don't be afraid," he said. "Take courage.
I am here!" Then Peter called to him, "Lord, if it's really
you, tell me to come to you, walking on the water."
"Yes, come," Jesus said. So Peter went over the side of the
boat and walked on the water toward Jesus. But when
he saw the strong wind and the waves, he was terrified
and began to sink. "Save me, Lord!" he shouted.*
MATTHEW 14:25–30 NLT

After Jesus had fed the five thousand, the disciples headed
homeward. Overnight, their boat ran into trouble on the tem-
peramental Sea of Galilee.

And that's when Jesus came to them, walking on the water.
What is this? A ghost? they wondered.

Jesus immediately comforted them with the truth.

Inspired, Peter asked to walk on the water to Jesus, and the
Lord allowed it. But once Peter realized what he was doing, he
lost his focus on Jesus. And down he went.

Would Jesus have allowed Peter on the water if He was not going to keep him safe? Hardly. The disciple should have known that. But fear overwhelmed his faith, and the water swept over his feet.

Like Peter, we may start out in a rush of faith. As we step out of the boat, we have no doubts. But when faith is challenged by the world, we begin to question our situation.

Just as Jesus would not allow Peter to drown, He will not let us go under either. If we understand that our life of faith is in the Lord's hands—and that our success comes from Him alone—we can walk on water. But once we focus on our situation and begin to doubt God's authority over our lives, we slip beneath life's waves.

Let's keep our eyes on Jesus so that we will *never* go under.

LORD, HELP ME KEEP MY EYES ON YOU AND LEAVE
FEAR BEHIND. YOU CONTROL MY WHOLE LIFE.

THE POWER OF LOVE

*Praise the LORD, all you nations. Praise him, all you people
of the earth. For his unfailing love for us is powerful;
the LORD's faithfulness endures forever. Praise the LORD!*
PSALM 117:1–2 NLT

What is as powerful as God's love? What else shows His control
over humanity more clearly?

Though we paid no attention to Him and walked far from
Him, God was not satisfied to let us remain separated from
Him, headed for destruction.

In human terms, it might seem easier (and even better) for
God to give up on a bad lot and let us receive the destruction
we earned. But God created and loved people, and the sacrifice
of salvation did not faze Him. Even from the earlier days of His
relationship with humanity, He made a covenant with Abram
that relied not on Abram but on His own faithfulness (Genesis
15). Through animal sacrifices, God provided a temporary way
out of sin that symbolized the death and propitiation that would
one day come through Jesus.

Satan believed that by drawing God's beloved humans into
sin he could destroy God's control over them. Clearly, the fallen
one had no understanding of the lengths God was willing to go

to in order to redeem humanity. The control that seemed to have slipped from His hands simply required a different solution.

Who could have foreseen a Savior who died for the sinner's wrongs? Even now, to those of us who are redeemed, it can be hard to fathom. When we look at our sin and the compassion He offers, we ask ourselves, *Why should God sacrifice Himself for me?*

Can you trust that God loved you enough to send His Son to die for you? Do you believe that this great price applies to all people who answer His call. . .and that there is no other way to approach Him? If so, praise Him for the power of His love and thank Him that He is still in control.

THANK YOU, LORD, FOR LOVING ME ENOUGH
TO TAKE MY SINS ON YOURSELF. I PRAISE
YOU FOR YOUR UNFAILING LOVE.

NO OTHER NAME

"For Jesus is the one referred to in the Scriptures, where it says, 'The stone that you builders rejected has now become the cornerstone.' There is salvation in no one else! God has given no other name under heaven by which we must be saved."

ACTS 4:11–12 NLT

Unbelievers reject the idea that God would command people to relate to Him through the sacrifice of Jesus and would deny salvation to those who believe anything else. Why shouldn't they be able to approach Him in any way they want? Aren't all gods equally valuable?

The answer is no. And here's why. . .

How could a God who really controlled His creation accept any purely human concept as a way to relate to Him? How could another faith that denies Jesus' deity and the value of His sacrifice do away with the consequences of sin?

We cannot have it both ways. Either God is in control or He isn't. And if we deny sin and the sacrifice for it, in our construct God becomes a weakling—because humanity controls salvation.

Jesus is the cornerstone, the squared-off rock that perfectly supports the building of faith. Because He alone holds up true faith, an unbeliever has no alternative. The ideas she puts in the place of Jesus will not stand on the day when God judges all people. Though those freethinking ideas may appear pleasing in a fallen world, they cannot stand against the powerful nature of God. One day, it will become clear how weak those concepts were and how unable they were to save anyone.

If we accept that God is in control, we need to trust in His way of salvation. Otherwise, we will fall for anything someone else claims will save. And then we will be trusting in a name that cannot save.

LORD, I KNOW YOUR NAME DESCRIBES YOUR
NATURE, AND NOTHING ELSE IS LIKE YOU.
I TRUST IN YOU ALONE. KEEP ME FROM WANTING
TO TRUST IN ANYONE OR ANYTHING ELSE.

UNWARY?

*The LORD is gracious and righteous; our God is
full of compassion. The LORD protects the unwary;
when I was brought low, he saved me.*

PSALM 116:5–6 NIV

Have you ever unwarily gotten into trouble—but then saw that trouble suddenly disappear? That wasn't a coincidence. Even when we are unaware of danger, God is not. We are His loved children, and He protects us from the unrighteous people who would put one over on us. Or if we do fall into trouble, He rescues us from it.

Are you on the brink of making a financial decision? Have you prayed about it, sought the advice of knowledgeable people, and read all the details carefully? If you still have a niggling doubt in the back of your mind, be careful. It may be God's Spirit giving you a warning. God doesn't encourage us to walk bravely into bad situations; we need to take care. But we can also rely on Him even if we get misled.

Were you about to make a job change that required a move and drastic changes in your life, then suddenly something happened? The job didn't come through or your circumstances changed so much that moving forward was out of the question.

You may feel sad about it, but don't despair. God may be redirecting your life away from a danger you could never have suspected. Years later, you may find out how He protected you, or you may never know why He changed things. Either way, know that God has a heavenly perspective. Let Him save you from your feelings of lowness because life didn't turn out as you expected, and trust that even better things are lying in the path you didn't prefer.

Nothing is outside God's hand, and we can trust that He will always bring us just what He has in mind for our lives.

THANK YOU, LORD, FOR PROTECTING ME FROM
UNSEEN TROUBLES THAT LIE AHEAD. EVEN IF YOU
TAKE ME DOWN AN UNEXPECTED PATH, I CAN TRUST
THAT YOU ARE SAVING ME, NOT HURTING ME.

WHO'S LEADING?

"Be strong and courageous. Do not be afraid or terrified because of them, for the LORD your God goes with you; he will never leave you nor forsake you. . . . Do not be afraid; do not be discouraged."
DEUTERONOMY 31:6, 8 NIV

Just as Israel was poised to cross the Jordan and enter their Promised Land, they faced a huge change: their leader, Moses, could not come with them. Because of his disobedience, Moses was not allowed to enter Canaan (Numbers 20:12; Deuteronomy 32:51–52). So God appointed Joshua as the new leader, and Moses died on Mount Nebo, overlooking the Promised Land.

Though they'd whined, complained, and fought with Moses, he was still the Hebrew people's prophet. Losing him must have been like losing the last familiar part of their old life.

Even before Joshua took over the leadership role, Moses answered Israel's most burning questions. What would they face as they crossed into their new land? How could they trust a new leader? Though the man who led them would be different, Moses reminded the people they would actually be following the Lord. Even as human leadership changed, God was not deserting them.

As the people followed His commands, they began to conquer their new turf. When they didn't trust Him, they faced troubles that could have been avoided.

If there are troubles in our lives, maybe it's because we're not allowing God to control us. Perhaps we've headed down our own paths instead of following His way. But He's always with us—He's promised never to leave or forsake us—so let's allow Him to lead. God already knows the potential pitfalls and the best way around them. There's no need for fear or discouragement.

LORD, HELP ME TO TURN FROM SIN AND WALK IN YOUR PATH EACH DAY. THEN I WILL KNOW YOU ARE IN CONTROL.

PURPOSE
BEHIND THE PAIN

The Lord of hosts has sworn, saying, "Surely, as I have intended,
so it shall come to pass, and as I have planned, so it shall stand.
. . . For the Lord of hosts has planned, and who can annul it?
And His hand is stretched out, and who can turn it back?"
Isaiah 14:24, 27 skjv

God had a plan: His people would be gobbled up by the Assyrian and Babylonian empires. Not a pleasant prospect for the Jews, who would suffer through the conquests. Yet God had a purpose behind the pain—that His people would appreciate Him and how good life had been when they followed Him. And they did come to that appreciation, as Psalm 137 shows. They wept for their homeland.

As His people suffered in the east, though, they still had the hope of return, for Isaiah 14:1 (niv) promised, "The Lord will have compassion on Jacob; once again he will choose Israel and will settle them in their own land." Even their disobedience could not disrupt God's plan. The day would come when these powerful enemies of God would be destroyed and lose their hold on His people. Though the reestablished nation of Israel would never reach the heights it had risen to under David and

Solomon, they would have their homeland back.

God has plans for nations and people. Those who seem powerful one day may be destroyed quickly. Those who are weakest may be raised up in His power.

Whatever He has in mind cannot be evaded. No one can annul His purposeful plan. As nations conspire together against God, their plans are thwarted (Psalm 2). One day, Jesus will rule over a heavenly inheritance, and sin's shackles will be broken.

For a time God's plans may seem to be failing. But we haven't seen the end of the story yet. Until then, as God's people, we live in hope.

LORD, I TRUST THAT YOUR PLANS WILL ALWAYS
COME TO PASS AND THAT THEY ARE ALWAYS GOOD.
UNTIL THE END, HELP ME TO BELIEVE IN YOU.

ALMIGHTY ONE

*David then took up residence in the fortress and called
it the City of David. He built up the area around it,
from the terraces inward. And he became more and more
powerful, because the LORD God Almighty was with him.*

2 SAMUEL 5:9–10 NIV

David was Israel's most successful king, though he had a long fight to come to the throne. Then he fought many enemies, including one of his own sons, to keep it.

Why did David gain so much power and wealth? Second Samuel tells us it was because God—"the LORD God Almighty"—was with him.

David become a powerful king because he believed in a powerful God. His strength arose not from himself but from His mighty God. Had David relied on his own strength, he would have failed utterly, as some of his disastrous mistakes show. A man who commits adultery and then murder to cover his tracks hardly appears to be good king material.

Despite his failures, David was a man after God's own heart (1 Samuel 13:14). He wasn't perfect—but when he failed, and failed miserably at times, his love for God did not end.

Do we see God as being bigger than we are? Or do we try

to bend God's will to our small ways? David had his moral failures, but he never lost sight of the fact that God was almighty, the final ruler. David always came to see that he was under God's command.

We, too, have our failures. Will they keep us from returning to God and remaining faithful to Him? Will the fact that God has not complied with our desires separate us from Him? Or will we put Him ahead of our wishes and recognize that power is only within the Almighty? When we do, we can expect to receive the power He gives to those He trusts.

LORD, KEEP ME FROM THINKING THAT YOU MUST
FULFILL ALL MY DESIRES. THEY ARE SO SMALL
COMPARED TO YOUR WILL. HELP ME TO SEEK YOUR
WILL AND WALK WITH YOU WHOLEHEARTEDLY.

ENDING REBELLION

Therefore, you kings, be wise; be warned, you rulers of the earth. Serve the LORD with fear and celebrate his rule with trembling.
PSALM 2:10–11 NIV

The idea that people should throw off the rule of God and rely on their own smarts is not a new one. Psalm 2 describes the attitude of politicians who do not value God or His laws. It also describes the results of that decision.

Those who seek freedom from God find themselves anything but free. For despite their opinions, the fact is that God created and rules all things. Plotting against Him is vain, and their success is impossible. They land in Satan's hands instead.

Like any ruler, God responds to rebellion. Though He has not immediately overthrown all who defy Him, it does not mean retribution won't come.

First, the Lord responds to the rebels with rebukes, not warfare (verse 5). God rarely reacts to disobedience with immediate destruction; instead, He offers time for repentance. But that's not His only response to rebels. One day the Son, His Messiah, "will break them with an iron rod and smash them like clay pots" (verse 9 NLT).

Though He may not rush to demolish His enemies, our Lord always remains in control.

What is true for nations can be true for individuals too. When Satan tempts us to see God as an overwhelming bully and to seek "freedom," we can look to passages like Psalm 2 and understand that He is nothing like that. He calls every rebel to lay down arms and seek Him, promising "joy for all who take refuge in him!" (verse 12 NLT).

LORD, HELP MY HEART NOT TO REBEL
AGAINST YOUR WILL IN MY LIFE.

REVAMPING THE EARTH

"Our Father in heaven, may your name be kept holy. May your Kingdom come soon. May your will be done on earth, as it is in heaven."
MATTHEW 6:9–10 NLT

Since God is all-powerful and holy, living in heaven, why does He care what happens on earth? Couldn't He just flick a finger and have everything the way He wants it?

Surely He could have made everything perfect and kept it that way. He could have destroyed the snake, Adam, and Eve to keep sin from invading this planet. But the one whose name is holy does not have that kind of character. He is not vicious but forgiving. He doesn't swat people out of existence for a single mistake but offers a way out of sin instead.

Far from what we might expect, God encourages us to take part in His regeneration of earth. We take part in showing the holiness of His nature through our lives. When His kingdom comes into our hearts, we begin our kingdom living, and our lives become testimonies to His willingness and ability to overcome sin in the sinner. Other people who might never have gone to church or heard a sermon have a chance to see God's work clearly.

As we pray the Lord's Prayer, we are not just asking God to work in the world. We commit to taking part too.

God's control of the earth is performed through His creation, His judgments, and also the people He created and saved. Of course, we do not have God's power—but as we work with Him, His Spirit moves in our lives to revamp the earth into a heavenly kingdom.

LORD, HELP ME TO WORK TOWARD YOUR GOALS AS YOUR SPIRIT TOUCHES MY LIFE. I WANT TO BE A PART OF YOUR WILL DONE PERFECTLY ON EARTH AS IT IS IN HEAVEN.

FORGIVEN

"Which is easier: to say to this paralyzed man, 'Your sins are forgiven,' or to say, 'Get up, take your mat and walk'? But I want you to know that the Son of Man has authority on earth to forgive sins." So he said to the man, "I tell you, get up, take your mat and go home." He got up, took his mat and walked out in full view of them all. This amazed everyone and they praised God, saying, "We have never seen anything like this!"
MARK 2:9–12 NIV

Four men were so concerned about getting healing for their friend that they ripped up a roof and lowered the man through the hole to Jesus. Instead of criticizing them for property damage, Jesus commended their faith and healed the man.

Jesus told the man his sins were forgiven, and that's when the trouble started. Some Pharisees who heard Him began to think, "He's blaspheming! Who can forgive sins but God alone?" (Mark 2:7 NIV).

Though they didn't have the courage to speak, Jesus knew their thoughts and took them to task. To prove His authority, He told the paralyzed man to get up and go home. The man rose, grabbed the mat he'd been lying on, and went his way.

Amazed, the watching people gave glory to God. But you

can bet the Pharisees were not happy.

In any group of people, you are likely to find doubters, those who do not believe Jesus has the authority He claims in scripture. The Pharisees didn't like seeing someone who contested their power. Did it ever cross their minds that Jesus really was who He said He was?

In a way, those grumbling Pharisees had something right: Who but God can forgive sins? They just didn't want Jesus to be God, the promised Messiah, the answer to all of this world's problems—but He was.

Today's doubters may not phrase their objections in the same way. But they also refuse to recognize the control God has over their lives. Let's never let them derail our faith.

LORD, I AM SO GLAD YOU FORGIVE SINS,
NO MATTER WHAT THE DOUBTERS THINK. THANK YOU
FOR FORGIVING MINE. I PRAISE YOUR NAME!

MY PASSOVER

The LORD keeps you from all harm and watches over your life. The LORD keeps watch over you as you come and go, both now and forever.
PSALM 121:7–8 NLT

Are you facing a challenging day? Feel confident in the fact that God watches over every minute of it. Whether you simply have too many tasks to fulfill in the next twenty-four hours or you face a terrible situation in life, nothing is outside God's knowledge or control.

We cannot go anyplace where God's control will fail us. We contend with no harm that He cannot rescue us from. Nothing in creation is beyond His reach or understanding.

We may often feel as if we control precious little in our lives. Our family or friends might not listen to us, for example—but we know God does.

Ah, we *know*. In our heads we've learned that this is true, but sometimes our hearts hesitate to believe it. As life pushes in on us, our knowledge may become threadbare. . .because intellectual assent is not enough. Faith and trust need to come alongside the scriptures we've memorized and the ideas we've learned in church.

Sometimes, God brings us into tough situations that make

our head knowledge more real. As we experience trials, we learn that God is more faithful than we expected.

After Israel experienced the Exodus, God frequently reminded His people to look back on that event and review where they had been and how He had been faithful in saving them. He even established Passover as a yearly reminder to His nation (Exodus 12:17).

Have you had a "Passover" in your life, a time when God kept or rescued you from harm? Remember it today and know that the Lord continues to keep you safe "both now and forever."

THANK YOU, LORD, FOR MY PASSOVERS. I TRUST
THAT YOU WILL KEEP ME FROM HARM TODAY
AND FOR ALL MY DAYS. MAY ANYTHING THAT
SEEMS LIKE HARM BE USED TO YOUR GLORY.

NEVER STRUCK DOWN

But we have this treasure in jars of clay to show that
this all-surpassing power is from God and not from us.
We are hard pressed on every side, but not crushed;
perplexed, but not in despair; persecuted, but not
abandoned; struck down, but not destroyed.

2 CORINTHIANS 4:7–9 NIV

The apostle Paul knew the difficulties Christians have when they feel weak and are living under pressure. This hero of the faith didn't have an easy time of it as he brought the gospel to his world. When people in Damascus wanted to kill him, he escaped by having his friends drop him over the city wall in a basket. During his missionary travels, he almost lost his life in a shipwreck. The churches he established sometimes supported him, but other times they made his life a misery. And he spent plenty of time under arrest by the Romans.

"Hard pressed" is a good description of Paul's life, yet all these troubles did not crush him. Through his ministry, the gospel spread westward, not stopped by his hardships.

Having a successful ministry does not mean life will always be smooth. The more successfully we spread God's message, the more the enemy may attack us. But though we are "jars of clay," the one who gave us the task is not. His is the power behind the mission, and He is the one who strengthens us. He will never abandon us. Whatever challenges we face, the Spirit is stronger than all of them.

Destruction is not our end. God may repurpose us throughout our years, and eventually we all die. But even death cannot destroy His goals. That's why we will share in Jesus' resurrection to eternal life.

No matter how crushed, perplexed, persecuted, or struck down we feel, God still controls our lives. He establishes the work we do and its scope. Satan cannot deflect that as long as we remain faithful to our Savior.

LORD, ALL MY STRENGTH LIES IN YOU. I PRAISE YOU FOR THE KINGDOM WORK YOU HAVE ACCOMPLISHED THROUGH MY LIFE. KEEP ME FAITHFUL EVERY DAY.

ETERNITY LIVING

"Woe to him who builds a city with bloodshed and establishes a town by injustice! Has not the LORD Almighty determined that the people's labor is only fuel for the fire, that the nations exhaust themselves for nothing? For the earth will be filled with the knowledge of the glory of the LORD as the waters cover the sea."
HABAKKUK 2:12–14 NIV

Look at the world stage, and doubts may fill your mind. Evil often seems to make headway on earth. Wrongdoing gets the most media attention. Fears fill our hearts as wars fill the world, and bloodshed and injustice seem to win.

But all that labor to gain land, money, or trade, which are usually the motives that cause wars, means nothing. Though it may last for a time, the evil ones wear themselves out for no reason. Earthly possessions look good now, but they never last. When you come down to it, nothing on earth continues for long. The city established today may disappear in a few hundred years. The work that seems so important now will mean nothing in a few years. But bloodshed and injustice are sins, and God repays sinners—if not now, then in eternal judgment.

One day, nothing of earthly importance will be as critical as it seems today. The prophet Habakkuk told of a day that outdoes all vigorous human effort, hands down. Then wrongdoing will end, and the world will be filled with the knowledge of God. Instead of a nation under God, we will be part of a world under God. Wickedness will be gone. Everyone in this perfect world will know God and praise Him. The New Jerusalem will be His alone. John described it as "the Holy City, Jerusalem, coming down out of heaven from God. It shone with the glory of God, and its brilliance was like that of a very precious jewel, like a jasper, clear as crystal" (Revelation 21:10–11 NIV).

What's important in your life today? Will it be important in eternity too?

LORD, HELP ME TO FOCUS ON THE THINGS THAT
ARE IMPORTANT IN YOUR KINGDOM. I DON'T
WANT TO WASTE MY DAYS ON EARTH.

SURROUNDED BY MOUNTAINS

As the mountains surround Jerusalem, so the LORD surrounds his people both now and forevermore.
PSALM 125:2 NIV

It might be surprising that the modern state of Israel has managed to hold on to its turf. A small nation of less than eleven thousand square miles and surrounded by enemies, this, the only democracy in the Middle East, has stood firm.

But Israel's people haven't done it on their own. Their planes and tanks and Iron Dome defense system were helpful, but they aren't truly Israel's protection.

God surrounds His nation and His people, protecting them as no military system can. And when He surrounds His people, they know they will be victorious. Human leadership is imperfect, but God has promised to protect the Jews and use them powerfully even through the end of this worldly life. One day He will draw many of them into faith in the Messiah.

Despite Jerusalem's history and the threat against His life there, Jesus felt tenderly toward the city: "Jerusalem, Jerusalem, you who kill the prophets and stone those sent to you, how often I have longed to gather your children together, as a hen gathers her chicks under her wings, and you were not willing" (Luke 13:34 NIV).

God continues to keep His promise to His people, even though they've resisted His Messiah. How certain we can be, as God's grafted-in people who have accepted Jesus, that He will surround us too! For surely, just as Jerusalem lies amid mountains, He protects all His people. And even if those mountains fell, it should not cause fear: "God is our refuge and strength, an ever-present help in trouble. Therefore we will not fear, though the earth give way and the mountains fall into the heart of the sea" (Psalm 46:1–2 NIV).

LORD, YOU ARE MY REFUGE IN ANY TROUBLE. WHEN FEAR STALKS MY HEART, REMIND ME OF YOUR PERFECT PROTECTION. THANK YOU FOR NEVER FAILING ME.

TWO SMALL COINS

While Jesus was in the Temple, he watched the rich people dropping their gifts in the collection box. Then a poor widow came by and dropped in two small coins. "I tell you the truth," Jesus said, "this poor widow has given more than all the rest of them. For they have given a tiny part of their surplus, but she, poor as she is, has given everything she has."
LUKE 21:1–4 NLT

These four verses are everything Luke tells us about the poor widow. At the end of her financial rope, she chose to put all her faith in God, giving Him all the money she had left. If that doesn't show faith that God is in control, what would?

The Old Testament makes it clear that the people of Israel were to take care of widows and orphans (Deuteronomy 14:29; 24:19–21) and that God would do the same (Psalm 146:9; Proverbs 15:25). No one was to take advantage of these disadvantaged people (Exodus 22:22).

Of course, Israel often failed to care for the neediest people of the land; we often see that in the prophets' condemnation of a nation gone far from God. But it was the will of God that His people be generous with their harvests, and He promised to be by the side of the widow.

Obviously, this widow of Jesus' day took those promises seriously. Though her coins were practically valueless, they were all she had. But she didn't hoard them. Perhaps because she felt as if she had little to lose, she gave it where it would have the most value. Jesus knew what she was doing and praised her for her commitment to God. For this woman, faith was all she had left, and she trusted that God would still be in control of her life without those two coins in her pocket.

When we have much more than that, do we trust Him with it? If we are barely making ends meet, have we put everything we have in God's hands?

LORD, HOW I USE MY MONEY SHOWS HOW MUCH
I TRUST YOU. PLEASE CONTROL ALL I HAVE.

AN INVITATION DECLINED

*Barak said to [Deborah], "If you go with me,
I will go; but if you don't go with me, I won't go."*
JUDGES 4:8 NIV

Deborah had a message from God for a military leader named Barak. She told the highly placed soldier that Israel's adversary was about to be defeated. Then Deborah delivered the most important part of the message she'd received: the Lord would "lead Sisera, the commander of Jabin's army, with his chariots and his troops to the Kishon River and give him into your hands" (Judges 4:7 NIV).

Barak had never heard of a more definite outcome. He hardly needed to fight—he only needed to be present. Barak should just be there to witness the victory. But he was no hero. Why? Because he declined to show up without moral support. He would go to battle only if Deborah joined him.

In that moment, God's plan remained good—He would deal with Israel's adversary. But the spotlight shifted from Barak to a woman named Jael. We might never have heard of Jael if Barak had accepted God's invitation to a ringside seat. Ultimately, it was Jael that God used to defeat the enemy.

God was in control from start to finish. This story proves

that when He asks us to be part of His plan and we turn Him down, God still gets what He wants. But a blessing meant for us will go to someone else.

Barak was undoubtedly blessed knowing that God had dealt with his country's foe. But don't you think he also regretted knowing that he had turned God down?

LORD, YOU HAVE POWER OVER EVERY ENEMY, HUMAN AND OTHERWISE. HELP ME TO TRUST AND OBEY YOU WHENEVER YOU CALL ME TO FIGHT.

IMPERFECT CONDITIONS

*But when Herod was dead, behold, an angel of the
Lord appeared in a dream to Joseph in Egypt, saying,
"Arise, and take the young Child and His mother, and
go into the land of Israel, for those who sought the young
Child's life are dead." And he arose, and took the young
Child and His mother, and came into the land of Israel.*

MATTHEW 2:19–21 SKJV

Though Mary and Joseph were glad to be safe, pagan Egypt
wasn't quite home. When God called them back to their native
land, Joseph never hesitated. He took Mary and Jesus and
returned to Israel.

Their trip to Egypt had been prophesied by Hosea (Hosea
11:1; Matthew 2:15). But that doesn't mean it was the most
comfortable time in the small family's life. They weren't living
in luxury, and they were separated from their closest friends.

Still, in all this, both Joseph and Mary remained where God
put them. They trusted that God had a plan and that nothing
had slipped out of His control.

Then on the night Joseph dreamed of the angel calling
them home, it was all worth it. How he and Mary must have
rejoiced. And how glad they must have been that they had
remained strong during the hard times.

We may wonder what God has in mind when we don't face perfect conditions in our lives. When we try to change something uncomfortable but all the doors seem barred against us, frustration may set in. Is *this* part of God's plan for our lives?

God didn't ask Mary and Joseph to take a pleasure cruise on the Nile, and He may well ask us to put up with less-than-ideal situations. It's not that He's stopped loving us—but we are here to serve Him, not the other way around. Eventually, faithful believers may be able to see beyond the discomforts they've been through to the plan God had all along.

LORD, HELP ME TO BE FAITHFUL EVEN
THROUGH THE UNCOMFORTABLE PARTS
OF MY LIFE. I WANT TO SERVE YOU.

NOT SHAKEN

Cast your cares on the LORD and he will sustain you; he will never let the righteous be shaken.

PSALM 55:22 NIV

Do you wonder if this verse is really true for you?

After all, shaking happens. The death of a loved one. The loss of a job. A relationship that doesn't work out. . . There are many moments in life when Christians can feel shaken. In fact, anyone who looks at life and decides its bad experiences are the be-all and end-all *will* feel shaken.

But the truth is this world is temporary. Just about everything changes. We can count on that.

We can also count on God.

Feelings can be good things, but they are not faith. And they can change so quickly that we don't know if we can trust ourselves or anyone else. Feelings should be more like servants in our lives than masters, because if we let them take control, we will be washed around like a tempest in a bucket. But faith in the Master is another matter. When we rely on Him, our emotions can be controlled. He gives us peace in the storm and pulls us out of the bucket. He may end the storm in a moment or over a period of time. But we won't be destroyed by the storm.

No matter how small our cares are, we can cast them on Him: "Cast all your anxiety on him because he cares for you" (1 Peter 5:7 NIV). We don't have to wait for the big stuff before we seek God's help. Even troubles in a teacup are important to Him because *we* are important to Him. He loves us so deeply, so completely.

Humbly cast your cares on Him, for the shaking lies under His command. Even if He doesn't remove a situation, He *will* sustain you.

LORD, I WANT TO BRING MY TROUBLES TO YOU NOW.
GIVE ME WISDOM TO DEAL WITH THEM, AND HELP
ME TRUST THAT YOU HAVE POWER OVER ALL.

BLANK CHECK

*He went away again the second time and prayed,
saying, "O My Father, if this cup may not pass away
from Me unless I drink it, Your will be done."*
MATTHEW 26:42 SKJV

Perhaps the most frightening part of the Lord's Prayer is Matthew 6:10 (NIV): "Your kingdom come, your will be done, on earth as it is in heaven." This prayer of submission opens the door to God's doing whatever He wants in our lives.

When we hand Him a blank check, what will He ask of us? How will our lives change?

Jesus clearly understood the fear surrounding this kind of prayer. In the garden of Gethsemane, He faced the greatest challenge—to give up His life for sinners and die a gruesome death on the cross, all for their salvation. In His humanity, He would have preferred another, gentler way and asked the Father to take the bitter cup from Him. But ultimately Jesus prayed "Your will be done" and headed for the cross.

Because He did that, when we pray "Your will be done," we know that Jesus has gone before us. When we approach God, it is as daughters whom He loves. Anything we are willing to do—however we open ourselves up to God—will bring good into our lives now or in His eternal kingdom.

All evil was placed on Jesus at the cross because He prayed for the Father's will to be done. And evil lost its ultimate power by His death and resurrection.

When we obey God and seek His will, we follow in Jesus' steps. As His sacrifice brought good into the world, anything God asks of us will also be of benefit to ourselves and others. Though we may face temporary pain, our submission brings about good—perhaps more of it than we know.

LORD, SOMETIME IT'S SCARY TO GIVE YOU A
BLANK CHECK. HELP ME TO TRUST IN YOUR LOVE
ENOUGH TO HAND OVER MY WHOLE LIFE.

SHEPHERD IN CONTROL

The LORD is my shepherd. I shall not want. He makes
me to lie down in green pastures. He leads me beside
the still waters. He restores my soul. He leads me in
the paths of righteousness for His name's sake.
PSALM 23:1–3 SKJV

Living life in the flock of the shepherd who controls our lives. . .
isn't this a peaceful picture?

The psalmist David understood what a good life for sheep
looked like, because his youth was spent tending a flock. Notice
that the sheep are in green pastures, not the dry desert. Calm
waters run through the pasture, providing deep drinks even
for lambs.

But David's picture of peaceful living doesn't end with having
enough to eat and drink—and this isn't about literal sheep
anyway. As his picture moves on to the spiritual peace humans
need, we recognize that *we* are God's sheep, and He cares for us.

If we feel that having God in control of our lives might
be a bit daunting, we need to carefully read Psalm 23. In the
shepherd's perfect world, we lack nothing, material or spiritual.
God gives us physical provision through food and drink, and
He offers rest too.

But that's not all our Lord offers. What could be better than a restored and righteous soul that never lacks any good thing? Our spirits need not be eaten up with doubts or worry. No worldly lions or bears destroy us.

Do you need soul restoration today? Turn to your shepherd, who controls both the physical realm and all things spiritual. He is waiting to restore your whole life.

LORD, YOU ARE SO GREAT AND POWERFUL—AND MAYBE
A BIT INTIMIDATING TOO. HELP ME TO REMEMBER THAT
YOU CARE FOR ME GENTLY, JUST LIKE A SHEPHERD.
YOU HAVE ONLY GOOD THINGS IN MIND FOR ME.

POWER FROM ABOVE

King Xerxes asked Queen Esther, "Who is he? Where is he—the man who has dared to do such a thing?" Esther said, "An adversary and enemy! This vile Haman!" Then Haman was terrified before the king and queen. . . . Then Harbona, one of the eunuchs attending the king, said, "A pole reaching to a height of fifty cubits stands by Haman's house. He had it set up for Mordecai, who spoke up to help the king." The king said, "Impale him on it!" So they impaled Haman on the pole he had set up for Mordecai. Then the king's fury subsided.
ESTHER 7:5–6, 9–10 NIV

Though it was dangerous, brave Queen Esther—who had not been summoned by the king for a whole month—approached her husband. She had a delicate issue to bring before Xerxes. By giving him information about how his favorite counselor, Haman, had plotted against her people, she was telling the king he had made a bad decision. He might not take it well, and their relationship wasn't strong enough for her to be certain he would side with her.

The queen carefully prepared her husband for the bad news by inviting him and Haman to two banquets. Finally Esther explained Haman's plot against her people.

Caught up in himself and utterly clueless, Haman thought he'd gained the queen's favor. But as soon as he heard the king ask who was behind the plot and heard the queen give the answer, he knew his goose was cooked. A short time later, this enemy of the Jews was dead.

When Esther went before the king, Haman looked very powerful. Her chances of success appeared slim. Though she wielded all her skills to save her people, a positive outcome remained uncertain.

Though God is never mentioned in Esther's book, He certainly took a hand in bringing down Haman. The deadly political situation created by a king's favorite was not as powerful as it seemed. The king's heart was still under God's control.

Do you have situations in which you feel powerless? None are beyond God's strength.

NOTHING IS BEYOND YOUR POWER IN MY LIFE, LORD.
PLEASE PROTECT ME WHEN I FEEL POWERLESS.

HONESTLY?

But there was a certain man named Ananias who, with his wife, Sapphira, sold some property. He brought part of the money to the apostles, claiming it was the full amount. With his wife's consent, he kept the rest. Then Peter said, "Ananias, why have you let Satan fill your heart? You lied to the Holy Spirit, and you kept some of the money for yourself. The property was yours to sell or not sell, as you wished. And after selling it, the money was also yours to give away. How could you do a thing like this? You weren't lying to us but to God!"

ACTS 5:1–4 NLT

As we read this passage, can we hear the foreboding music in the background? Or do we write this couple's actions off and wonder what the big deal is?

Ananias sold his property. No problem. If he'd given generously of his money, that would have been no problem either. But when he came to give the apostles his purported gain, he never expected that Peter would know how much he'd sold the property for. Wanting to seem more generous than he was, he claimed he'd given everything.

How could anyone catch him in his lie?

Whether God revealed the sale price or Peter heard from another source, the Lord saw to it that the apostle got the information. What a shock it must have been to Ananias—and to Sapphira, when she came to Peter later and was complicit in the lie. God made an example of both as they fell to the floor, dead.

They had lied to Peter, yes. More importantly, they had lied to God.

Honestly, how did they think they could keep the truth from God? Did they forget He is omniscient?

But do *we* ever try to lie to God? We may not do so as publicly as this couple, and we may not be outed the way they were—but be sure that God knows, and the truth may still catch up to us in the end. He's always aware of what we do and think.

Yes, that's a warning—but it's also a reminder of the love and concern God has for each of us. When we honor and obey Him, God turns every bit of His power to our benefit.

LORD, MAY I ALWAYS BE HONEST WITH YOU.

MINISTRY TRUTHS

*"You didn't choose me. I chose you. I appointed you to
go and produce lasting fruit, so that the Father will
give you whatever you ask for, using my name."*
JOHN 15:16 NLT

. . . .

As Jesus prepared Himself for the crucifixion, He also readied
His disciples for the changes they would face. When they stepped
out in ministry without the Master physically by them, they
would need confidence in their mission and in the knowledge
that God remained with them. So in John 15 Jesus gave them
a short course in Christian ministry.

Jesus described the relationship between the Father, Himself,
and every believer this way: "I am the true grapevine, and my
Father is the gardener. He cuts off every branch of mine that
doesn't produce fruit, and he prunes the branches that do bear
fruit so they will produce even more" (John 15:1–2 NLT).

When someone comes to God, it is God, not the person,
who does the choosing—the Lord is the one who calls people
to Himself. He has a purpose for the life of each believer, and
He is behind each ministry that He gives. And through God's
own power, each ministry fulfills His work on earth. God chose
us to produce certain kinds of fruit for His kingdom. As we

step out in faith to complete our mission, the Father provides all the tools we need when we ask in the name of the Son.

Our successes do not come easy. Just as His enemies fought Jesus, the enemies of God and His Word will trouble us (see John 15:18–20). Yet they cannot be victorious over the Lord who lies behind the whole mission of bringing salvation to the world.

LORD, I THANK YOU FOR CHOOSING ME AND BRINGING ME TO FAITH IN YOU. I COULD NEVER HAVE DONE THAT ON MY OWN. GIVE ME CONFIDENCE THAT YOU ARE IN CHARGE OF THE MINISTRY YOU PLACE BEFORE ME AND THAT YOU WILL BRING IT TO FRUITION IN YOUR OWN TIME AND WAY.

HELP IN TROUBLE

God is our refuge and strength, always ready to help in times of trouble. So we will not fear when earthquakes come and the mountains crumble into the sea. Let the oceans roar and foam. Let the mountains tremble as the waters surge!
PSALM 46:1–3 NLT

When we face dangers in our lives, can we trust that God is always ready to help? If the earth seems to shatter below our feet and the sea overwhelms us, can we grab on to God in faith, or do we seek some other support?

Shattering experiences may not be physical earthquakes. Life has many destructive physical and spiritual experiences: serious illnesses, loss of loved ones, a favorite job that suddenly becomes difficult, relationships ended abruptly, a church destroyed by sin. The list is endless.

No matter if we face some sort of worldly destruction or a spiritual challenge, in times of trouble it seems our lives are tossed up in the air, leaving no firm footing.

Psalm 46 tells us we need not fear *when*, not *if*, earthquakes come. We can expect troubles to enter our lives. No person of faith has a constantly smooth existence. Look at Paul, a faithful man who served God with every fiber of his being. If anyone "deserved" a peaceful life, it was this apostle. Yet he went from one challenge to another—*and* he impacted the world for Christ as no one else did.

If we try to gauge the success of our Christian life by its peacefulness, we'll get it wrong. God doesn't use that measuring stick to identify a strong believer. He judges our lives by our faithfulness in turning to Him in every situation.

When troubles seem ready to destroy our lives, do we faithfully seek our refuge and strength? Do we trust that He will always help?

He will, though perhaps not in the way we expect.

LORD, HELP ME TO COME TO YOU WITH EVERY NEED,
TRUSTING THAT YOU ALWAYS WANT TO AND WILL HELP.

IMPOSSIBLE CONDITIONS

*"What do you want me to do for you?" Jesus asked.
"My Rabbi," the blind man said, "I want to see!" And Jesus
said to him, "Go, for your faith has healed you." Instantly
the man could see, and he followed Jesus down the road.*
MARK 10:51–52 NLT

Blind Bartimaeus wanted to be healed so badly that when he heard that Jesus was passing by, he made a racket, calling out to Him and begging for mercy. The "proper" people around him were embarrassed and tried to shush Bartimaeus. *Is this a good way to meet the Master?* they probably thought. But their objections only made Bartimaeus cry out all the louder.

Jesus heard the man's cries and stopped. "Call him," He told His disciples (Mark 10:49 NIV). The blind man sprang up and went to Jesus.

Bartimaeus had lots of faith. But he could not heal himself. He knew his own limitations and the depth of his need. Anyone who looked at him could see what his problem was. No matter what help he'd sought before or how little or much he'd gotten, it had failed. The blind man thoroughly recognized his hopeless condition. But Jesus was the one who could change it. Letting this opportunity for healing pass him by was unthinkable.

Like Bartimaeus, we may find ourselves in impossible conditions. No one seems able to help. We've tried everything, unsuccessfully. Do we despair and give up? Doubt that anyone, even God, cares?

We are mistaken if we doubt that God cares and is willing and able to help. We need to call out to Jesus. He may seem to be passing us by, but a prayer as determined as the blind man's cry and a few steps will bring us to His side.

There was no question that Jesus, the divine Savior, could heal Bartimaeus. Why do we question that He can heal our lives too?

LORD, I NEED YOUR HEALING IN MY LIFE. I CRY OUT
FOR YOUR MERCY. OPEN MY EYES TO YOUR WILL.

SAFE FROM FIRE

Shadrach, Meshach, and Abed-nego answered and said to the king, "O Nebuchadnezzar, we are not anxious to answer you in this matter. If it be so, our God whom we serve is able to deliver us from the burning fiery furnace. And He will deliver us out of your hand, O king. But if not, let it be known to you, O king, that we will not serve your gods, nor worship the golden statue that you have set up."
DANIEL 3:16–18 SKJV

Is there any greater testimony of faith than the answer these three Jews gave King Nebuchadnezzar, who tried to force them into idolatry? No matter the consequences, they would not bow the knee to an idol—even one that the king himself had commanded to be made.

As they took their stand, these Jews knew they were setting up a situation that could cause their deaths—yet they trusted in God more than the Babylonian king who had conquered their land and brought them into his kingdom. To the world, it must have seemed the conquering king had more power than God. After all, God hadn't intervened and kept Nebuchadnezzar from winning the battle. But these men knew better.

Though their lives seemed to lie in the hands of a powerful

pagan king, Shadrach, Meshach, and Abed-nego knew they were truly under God's control. Without faith in Him, what would they have left? Separation from God is the most painful experience imaginable. So instead of settling for an earthly king's favor and riches, they stood their ground.

Lots of Sunday school kids can tell the end of the story: The king had the young men thrown in the fire, but it never touched them. Their salvation caused Nebuchadnezzar to understand the power of God.

If God saved these three men from the hottest fire, are there any fires He cannot protect us from?

LORD, I WANT TO STAND FIRM FOR YOU.
SAVE ME FROM THE FIRES IN MY LIFE.

IN THE LIONS' DEN

Now when Daniel knew that the writing was signed, he went to his house, and—his windows being open in his room toward Jerusalem—he knelt on his knees three times a day and prayed and gave thanks before his God, as he did formerly. Then these men assembled and found Daniel praying and making supplication before his God. Then they came near and spoke before the king concerning the king's decree: "Have you not signed a decree that every man who asks a petition of any god or man within thirty days, except of you, O king, shall be thrown into the den of lions?" The king answered and said, "It is true, according to the law of the Medes and Persians, which does not alter."

DANIEL 6:10–12 SKJV

Daniel was such a good leader that King Darius placed him at the top of his government, over the newly appointed presidents and princes.

Jealous, those leaders of Babylon plotted to get rid of him. Seeking a flaw in Daniel, they found none. So this opposition party got their king to sign a law that said that for thirty days anyone who worshiped anyone except the king would die.

Knowing the law had been established, Daniel didn't give

up worshiping God—just as his enemies had expected. They leaped to bring his worship to the king's attention, and the king could do nothing. He couldn't revoke any duly enacted law. Though he sought a way to free Daniel from this trap, Darius failed. The conspirators seemed to have won as Daniel was brought to the lions' den.

The sleepless king spent the night fasting. In the morning, when the king went to the den, Daniel's voice rose to him, announcing that his God had shut the lions' mouths. He remained unharmed.

In the end, the conspirators and their families took Daniel's place in the den and did not fare so well. And Darius? He commanded that all his people were to fall before the Lord and praise Him!

Have you ever had trouble with a jealous enemy? There's no reason to lose heart. Standing firm in God is your best choice, for He protects His faithful children (Psalm 55:22).

LORD, THANK YOU FOR PROTECTING
ME WHEN OTHERS ATTACK.

THE PRAISE SOLUTION

Though you have made me see troubles, many and bitter, you will restore my life again; from the depths of the earth you will again bring me up. You will increase my honor and comfort me once more.

PSALM 71:20–21 NIV

Does trouble overwhelm you? Has God shown you "many and bitter" troubles?

Remember that *God* has shown them to you. Though you may not yet understand the troubles, nothing you have gone through is purposeless, because none of it is beyond His control or plan. God hasn't left you in the lurch. "For you have been my hope, Sovereign LORD," the psalmist said (Psalm 71:5 NIV).

God may design part of our lives with pain and suffering. In that moment it's up to us to choose faith or doubt.

Darkness may seem to cover us for a while. But Jesus said, "I am the light of the world. Whoever follows me will never walk in darkness, but will have the light of life" (John 8:12 NIV). Though at times our light of faith may feel like a flickering candle, we do not walk in total darkness as long as we protect that flame. Only if we despair and lose faith do we lack light. But even if we turn our backs on God, He never walks away from us. He may allow us to feel our own emptiness for a time, but only to draw us back to Him in the end.

When we will not walk with Him, we do not face the light of Jesus; we peer into the darkness experienced by those who do not know Him. Yet the light is just behind us. We see it when we turn in faith to Him.

Despite all his troubles, this psalmist considered his situation and turned to God. Psalm 71 ends with a song of praise recognizing the God who delivered him. Praise neutralized the fears that darkened his life.

LORD, HELP ME TO TRUST THAT EVEN MY PAINFUL MOMENTS ARE IN YOUR HANDS. HELP ME TO TURN TO YOU IN PRAISE.

PEACE PRESCRIPTION

The LORD established the kingdom under his control; and all Judah brought gifts to Jehoshaphat, so that he had great wealth and honor. His heart was devoted to the ways of the LORD; furthermore, he removed the high places and the Asherah poles from Judah.

2 CHRONICLES 17:5–6 NIV

Why did the kings of Israel and Judah have such a hard time understanding that blessings came from following the Lord? So often, when they slid away into idolatry, these nations suffered; yet both the people and the kings seemed determined to set up even more idols for worship.

Jehoshaphat inherited the throne of Judah and strengthened the military outposts. It was a time of blessing for the king: he successfully controlled his new kingdom and received wealth and honor. As the king arranged for the people to learn the Law by sending out teachers, his reign blessed his nation, and there was peace. "The fear of the LORD fell on all the kingdoms of the lands surrounding Judah, so that they did not go to war against Jehoshaphat" (2 Chronicles 17:10 NIV). Judah became powerful (verses 12–13) because God was in control through a king who loved Him.

It's the same in our lives. Peace rules when we have good leadership that loves and serves God, whether it's in our nation or in corporate boardrooms. And in our personal lives, when we habitually seek God's will and serve Him, we can have peace in the face of persistent trouble.

Are you looking for peace? Then make sure your life is integrated with God's will. Though we cannot control the rest of the world, we can keep our hearts connected to Jesus.

Idols may seem appealing for a time, but they only bring sorrow. Know the Word of God and follow it—and peace will fill your heart.

KEEP ME FROM THE IDOLS OF THIS WORLD, LORD. MAY I LIVE DEEPLY IN YOUR WORD AND DAILY SEEK YOUR FACE.

WHO'S IN CONTROL?

Just as you used to offer yourselves as slaves to impurity and to ever-increasing wickedness, so now offer yourselves as slaves to righteousness leading to holiness. When you were slaves to sin, you were free from the control of righteousness. What benefit did you reap at that time from the things you are now ashamed of? Those things result in death!

ROMANS 6:19–21 NIV

....

Before we knew Jesus, perhaps we felt we were in control of our lives—but it was all an illusion.

Scripture makes it clear that we have only two options: we can be slaves to God and His righteousness or slaves to sin and Satan.

Before we knew Jesus, we fell victim to every sin that slipped into our lives. Resist as we might—and, truthfully, we didn't resist very much—we could not put holiness into our hearts. When we did good, it was because it made us feel good or otherwise benefited us. Though we may even have looked like "nice people," sin marred our lives, and we had no way to change that. Righteousness was far from us.

Once we recognized our desperate situation and came to Jesus, He gave us a new nature, one that seeks holiness through

Him. Now, as God's bond servants, we willingly become new people who improve in holy living. We can do that because the Holy Spirit controls our lives.

That control is not a dictatorship. Though the Spirit lives in us, He does not force us to turn from sin. Of course, when we disobey, we will feel His loving discipline. He will teach us through our experiences. And as we follow Him, love Him, and experience the blessings of His forgiveness, we will desire to serve Him more and more.

The enemy of our Lord is also our enemy. Sin still pulls at us, and our part of the God-human relationship is to confess and turn from sin when it begins to charm us. Once God is in control again, our lives feel blessed.

LORD, TAKE CONTROL OF MY LIFE. HELP ME TO WALK CONSISTENTLY WITH YOU AND SERVE YOU EACH DAY.

SELF-CONTROL

"You will be accepted if you do what is right. But if you refuse to do what is right, then watch out! Sin is crouching at the door, eager to control you. But you must subdue it and be its master."
GENESIS 4:7 NLT

. . . .

Cain gave God a sacrifice from his harvest, but God refused the gift and the giver. Afterward, God confronted Cain for his anger and warned that sin crouched before him, waiting to take control. "Fight back and master your emotions," He essentially warned Cain.

Cain isn't the only one who has fought this fight. We've all felt the tug of jealousy when someone else gets what we want. Few of us, thankfully, will ever respond to Cain's extreme.

But sin still crouches at our doors. The temptation to let our hurts fuel negative actions and words may feel impossible to resist, but God's advice to Cain tells us it isn't. If we fuel our anger, it grows and destroys us. But if we seek to subdue wrong thoughts and feelings in Christ, we can have victory over them. This is hard spiritual work, but victory comes through the Spirit.

Satan or God will control our lives. We have a lot of say over who is in charge. We cannot cede control to the enemy and take no blame for what happens. Over and over, scripture calls us to exert self-control in our spiritual lives and to put our thinking and feeling under Jesus' control: "So prepare your minds for action and exercise self-control. Put all your hope in the gracious salvation that will come to you when Jesus Christ is revealed to the world" (1 Peter 1:13 NLT).

Remember, though we can and should ask God to control our lives, that doesn't mean we sit back and expect Him to do everything. We are working *with* Him. When we do, His control will shine through our faith.

LORD, AS YOU CONTROL MY LIFE,
HELP ME TO ACTIVELY RESIST SIN.

STILL IN COMMAND

And when He had entered into a ship, His disciples followed Him. And behold, there arose a great tempest in the sea, to such an extent that the ship was covered with the waves. But He was asleep. And His disciples came to Him and awoke Him, saying, "Lord, save us! We are perishing."
MATTHEW 8:23–25 SKJV

. . . .

When the disciples were in trouble, they knew who to call on. Though it may have seemed odd that Jesus was sleeping soundly through a tempest, they still trusted that He had a solution to their problem.

Perhaps they weren't quite perishing; after all, they were still in the boat. But a ship covered with waves may not stay afloat for long. Before their vessel was gone and they were in the water, it was time to seek help. They woke Jesus.

Though waves covered their ship, Jesus responded, "Why are you fearful, O you of little faith?" (Matthew 8:26 SKJV). Jesus was not unwilling to help, but first, He turned the disciples' thoughts in the proper direction.

Had the Twelve been deeper into their ministry, they might have understood that God was not going to desert His Son amid a storm. With Jesus they were safe. And God had a plan for the disciples that would never come to pass if they drowned in the Sea of Galilee. Surely Jesus was aware of all this. If they'd really been threatened, He would have acted immediately. Even a need for sleep would not have kept Him from dealing with danger.

But the disciples' fear had overwhelmed their faith.

Jesus stepped in to rebuke the wind and waves, and the disciples began to understand His incredible power.

Like the disciples, we face storms that bring fear to our hearts. But we can be certain that God's power has not been removed from our lives. He still protects us, and we see that as we trust in Him. He is still in the boat, still in command.

LORD, I THANK YOU THAT YOUR POWER IS ALWAYS
PROTECTING ME. YOU ARE AWARE OF ALL MY
TROUBLES. YOU ARE NEVER ASLEEP AT THE HELM.

NO TURNING BACK

At this point many of his disciples turned away and deserted him. Then Jesus turned to the Twelve and asked, "Are you also going to leave?" Simon Peter replied, "Lord, to whom would we go? You have the words that give eternal life. We believe, and we know you are the Holy One of God."
JOHN 6:66–69 NLT

When Jesus began to teach about His being the Bread of Life, many of His disciples walked out on Him. It seemed impossible that Jesus—the carpenter's son, as they thought—could be the Messiah.

Jesus turned to the Twelve and asked if they, too, would leave. Now was the time for them to make a choice, and Peter stepped forward to declare their faith. What other options did they have? Knowing He was sent by God, could they return to the unsatisfying teachings of the scribes and Pharisees? Where would that get them? They had seen God's power in Jesus, and anything less would be valueless.

Nothing in this world replaces the truths of God. When His teachings get challenging, some may seek alternatives that seem more comfortable, but they will never be satisfied with less than the real thing. Anyone who walks away from Him will never be at peace. Having put our lives in God's hands, there is no turning back.

The unfaithful followers of Jesus missed out on so much. God's guidance may have been absent throughout their lives because they could not commit to His Son. Or perhaps they came to faith in Jesus later, after His death, and understood how much they had missed out on.

Either we recognize Jesus as Savior and commit our lives to Him, or we refuse to put our lives in His hands. There is no halfway point. Only those who fully commit receive the blessings of His love.

LORD, I COMMIT MY LIFE TO YOU COMPLETELY.
WHO ELSE CAN I TURN TO?

KEYS TO THE KINGDOM

God saved you by his grace when you believed.
And you can't take credit for this; it is a gift from
God. Salvation is not a reward for the good things
we have done, so none of us can boast about it.
EPHESIANS 2:8–9 NLT

Coming to Christ is a wonderful thing, whether it happens slowly or in a moment. But one thing is sure: it's not something that happens because *we* design it. Though we may feel a need for salvation, we cannot cause it to happen. No matter how much we try to gain access to God, we cannot accomplish it. He alone chooses His people, calling them to Himself (Matthew 11:27; Romans 8:28; 9:15–16).

God's grace lies behind His call. He offers salvation to all, but not all come. Those who determinedly resist His Spirit's call remain in their sins. Those who humbly answer the pull of the Spirit find salvation. But none of us can micromanage our way into the kingdom. If God did not call us, we would never make our way there.

None of us are good enough to take credit for our own salvation. Through His perfect Son, Jesus, God gifts us with it. When sin distanced us from the perfect God, He made a way for us to approach Him; but apart from the Spirit, our arms cannot reach God. And apart from the sacrifice of Jesus, we cannot be made whole.

If we begin to take pride in the idea that we came to Jesus, let us reconsider the truth. We can come to Him only because He calls. His was the first action, and we responded to His grace. We could not enter a kingdom to which we had no keys. The keys to the gates of heaven belong to God, and we cannot enter any other way.

God never gives us heaven as a reward for our deeds. If He rewarded us for what we've earned, we'd have a place in hell. His mercy and grace, not our pride, placed us in His kingdom.

I WORSHIP YOU, LORD, FOR YOUR MERCY
AND GRACE IN SAVING ME.

BEST WILL

*"From the day I brought my people Israel out of Egypt,
I have never chosen a city among any of the tribes of Israel as
the place where a Temple should be built to honor my name.
But I have chosen David to be king over my people Israel."*

1 KINGS 8:16 NLT

God had chosen David to rule as king over His people, there was no doubt of that. He'd blessed David and given him the throne, taking it away from King Saul. David overcame Saul and other enemies, and God called David "a man after my own heart" (Acts 13:22 NLT).

Yet it was not God's will for David to achieve his greatest desire, to build God a temple in Jerusalem (1 Kings 8:18–19).

David had been a man of warfare. That was the role God gave him and helped him to succeed in. But it was not His will for David also to build the temple. Under this king's hands a great palace had been built, but temple building was the job of David's son and heir, Solomon, who would live in peace.

Though disappointed when the news was announced to him, David accepted God's will. Then the king worshiped God for all He had done for him (2 Samuel 7).

David understood, by faith, that God had a certain calling

for him. There was work for him to do for God's kingdom and there was work for another. Generously, instead of building the temple, he helped his son prepare for the moment the work would begin, gathering the materials and encouraging Israel's leaders to support Solomon in the work (1 Chronicles 22).

Is there a spiritual work on your heart? Draw near to God and pray. But if He tells you to support another in the work, take David as an example. Without bitterness, support the one God gave the work to. His will is always the best.

LORD, SHOW ME THE WORK YOU HAVE FOR ME, AND
HELP ME SUPPORT OTHERS IN THEIRS TOO.

CHOSEN

*Again, Jesse made seven of his sons pass before Samuel. And
Samuel said to Jesse, "The L*ORD *has not chosen these." And
Samuel said to Jesse, "Are all your children here?" And he said,
"There still remains the youngest, and behold, he is keeping
the sheep." And Samuel said to Jesse, "Send and bring him
here, for we will not sit down until he comes." And he sent
and brought him in. Now he was ruddy and moreover had
a beautiful face and was good-looking. And the L*ORD *said,
"Arise, anoint him, for this is he." Then Samuel took the horn
of oil and anointed him in the midst of his brothers. And the
Spirit of the L*ORD *came on David from that day forward.*

1 SAMUEL 16:10–13 SKJV

The prophet Samuel looked over seven of Jesse's sons, seeking
the one God wanted to crown the king of His people. None
of the men who stood before him passed the test.

Then a thought came to the prophet. *Are these all of Jesse's sons?*

No, Jesse told him. He had a younger son who was out watching the sheep—a dirty, lowly, and sometimes dangerous job.

As soon as David came into Samuel's presence, the Lord told
the prophet he'd found the right one. Samuel anointed David
immediately, right in front of the brothers who were not chosen.

God doesn't always choose the obvious person for an important job. Jesse may have thought his eldest son was the one, but he wasn't. As Samuel met each successive son, Jesse probably felt perplexed. What was wrong with each? Did the prophet have it right? Then the youngest being chosen must have been a shock. Was David ready to be king? What credentials did a shepherd have?

But David was just who God wanted and needed—a lowly shepherd for His people.

We may consider ourselves the most unlikely candidates for God's kingdom or His service. Maybe we are the youngest or least gifted in our families, yet God chooses us to serve Him. Surely He has a plan, and through His Spirit He will make us successful.

THANK YOU, LORD, FOR CHOOSING ME TO DO YOUR WORK.
HELP ME TO DO IT FAITHFULLY AND SUCCESSFULLY.

UNMOVED

*He will not allow your foot to be moved; He who keeps
you will not slumber. Behold, He who keeps Israel shall
neither slumber nor sleep. The LORD is your keeper.
The LORD is your shade on your right hand.*

PSALM 121:3–5 SKJV

Are you tempted to think God's asleep on the job? Maybe your
life isn't heading where you expected, and no matter how much
you pray or try to change things, nothing gets better.

God is not asleep.

Remember His people's history? He brought the nation of
Israel under Joshua's command, destroyed her enemies, then
allowed His people to be dispersed and re-formed twice. Israel
became an independent nation again after World War II, a
devastating conflict that included a massive attempt to wipe
out the Jews. Today, God is still caring for His people, both
Jew and Gentile. He is the keeper who protects those whom
He loves, even those who rejected the Messiah.

Psalm 121:3 says that God won't allow your foot to "be
moved." Perhaps He is holding you in place for a time because
you were trying to step in the wrong direction. There are moments
when God wants you just where you are. Perhaps the job possibility

that looks so appealing or the relationship that draws your heart would be disastrous. Or it could be that God is helping you stand firm in the place where He wants you to work for His kingdom.

We can't always know what's best. We do not see the future—the job that will not be there in a year, when we'll really need it, or the relationship that will cause nothing but heartache.

Whatever happens, you can count on this: Anything He brings into your life will be better than you expected. And anything He does not give you is something less than the best, which He did not want in your life.

God is in control. And even if life isn't exactly what you expected, He is being good to you.

LORD, I GIVE MY LIFE TO YOU, INCLUDING
ALL MY EXPECTATIONS AND DESIRES.
HELP ME TO LIVE IN YOUR WILL.

UNUSUAL PROVISION

*Jesus said to him first, "What do you think, Simon?
From whom do the kings of the earth take custom or tribute?
From their own children or from strangers?" Peter said to
Him, "From strangers." Jesus said to him, "Then the children
are free. However, lest we should offend them, go to the sea
and cast a hook, and take up the first fish that comes up.
And when you have opened its mouth, you shall find a piece
of money. Take that and give it to them for Me and you."*
MATTHEW 17:25–27 SKJV

The idea of God the Father extracting a temple tax from
His own Son is unthinkable, as Jesus pointed out to His
disciple Peter.

The temple tax collectors had cornered Peter, wanting to
know if Jesus paid that tax. Since Peter had assured them He
did, Jesus made good on His follower's word.

As the ultimate high priest, Jesus would have been exempt
from the tax. All priests were exempt from this tax that paid for
the upkeep of the temple. But of course, to the tax collectors—
who did not believe in Jesus and would never have accepted
that He was God and priest—this would merely have seemed
like an unusual way to slip out of paying the tax. To start the

argument would have gotten them nowhere, even if Peter had had a fuller idea of who Jesus was.

Though Jesus frequently confronted the scribes and Pharisees, in this instance He sought not to offend anyone and told Peter to pay the tax. He even gave His disciple a unique way to find the money: Peter was to use his skills as a fisherman and catch a fish. In its mouth he would find God's provision.

God provided for Peter, even though he had promised this payment carelessly. And God provides for us, too, in spite of our own errors or misunderstandings. Our failings do not keep Him from being faithful, compassionate, and in control.

LORD, I THANK YOU THAT NOTHING KEEPS YOU
FROM PROVIDING FOR ALL MY NEEDS.

WELL-PLACED TRUST

"And this is the writing that was written: MENE, MENE, TEKEL, UPHARSIN. This is the interpretation of it. MENE: God has numbered your kingdom and finished it. TEKEL: You are weighed in the balances and are found lacking. PERES: Your kingdom is divided and given to the Medes and Persians." Then Belshazzar gave the command, and they clothed Daniel with scarlet and put a chain of gold around his neck and made a proclamation concerning him, that he should be the third ruler in the kingdom.
DANIEL 5:25–29 SKJV

During a banquet in which King Belshazzar wanted to impress his thousand guests, he had the vessels from the temple in Jerusalem brought in to use as drinking bowls. Surely his banquet became impressive, though not in the way he expected. As his guests drank down their wine and worshipped their idols, a man's hand appeared and wrote strange words on the wall—words that no one could understand until the prophet Daniel was called to interpret them. Daniel 5:25–28 records Daniel's interpretation—not a very upbeat message.

Standing before Belshazzar, Daniel was in a difficult spot. Speaking the truth was dangerous, especially before this court full of Belshazzar's supporters. And though Daniel had been in favor during Nebuchadnezzar's reign, Belshazzar remembered nothing about Daniel until the queen brought this prophet to his attention.

From a place of weakness Daniel had to speak judgment to a powerful king.

Daniel didn't hesitate. Crisply, he announced the king's doom—and got rewarded for it.

Doubtless the king's approval meant little to Daniel compared to his service to his God. In fact, Daniel had turned down Belshazzar's promised reward before he even interpreted the message. As it turned out, the king's promises wouldn't have lasted long, as Belshazzar was killed that very night. Yet the new king, Darius the Mede, improved on Belshazzar's reward. He put Daniel at the head of the realm.

Faithfulness to God does not always come without risks. Yet our trust in the God who controls all things is never misplaced. It wasn't so for Daniel, and it cannot be for us either.

LORD, I PLACE MY TRUST IN YOU.
I KNOW YOU WILL NEVER FAIL ME.

LARGE NEEDS

*Then Joshua spoke to the LORD on the day when the LORD
delivered up the Amorites before the children of Israel, and
he said in the sight of Israel: "Sun, stand still on Gibeon,
and you, Moon, in the Valley of Aijalon." And the sun stood
still, and the moon stayed, until the people had avenged
themselves of their enemies. Is this not written in the Book
of Jashar? So the sun stood still in the midst of heaven and
did not hasten to go down for about a whole day. And there
was no day like that before it or after it, when the LORD
listened to the voice of a man, for the LORD fought for Israel.*
JOSHUA 10:12–14 SKJV

. . . .

After the Israelites moved into the Promised Land and conquered
Ai, King Adoni-zedek became concerned about the dangers of
these invaders. He put together an alliance of Amorite city-states
to attack Gibeon, a city that had made peace with Joshua and
his people. When Gibeon called on Israel for help, Joshua and
his troops responded.

The Lord took part in the resulting battle, confusing the
enemy and raining down huge hailstones on them. The Amorites
and their allies ran. God's soldiers followed them, but as night
came, Joshua asked something unusual. He needed daylight to

follow Israel's enemies, so would God make the sun and moon stand still while they finished the job? And "the LORD listened to the voice of a man, for the LORD fought for Israel."

Do we have something big we'd like to ask God for, yet we hesitate to come before Him in prayer?

Doesn't God fight for us too? And through Him can't we win all our spiritual battles? Though we may not ask Him to stop the sun in its course, we can ask for the fulfillment of large needs. Matthew 7:7 tells us to ask and it will be given to us. But if we fear asking, our desires may never be ours. We need to come to the King for all we need.

LORD, HELP ME TO BRING LARGE NEEDS TO YOU AND
TO SEEK WHATEVER BRINGS GLORY TO YOU.

AWESTRUCK

*God also said to Abraham, "As for Sarai your wife, you are
no longer to call her Sarai; her name will be Sarah. I will
bless her and will surely give you a son by her. I will bless
her so that she will be the mother of nations; kings of peoples
will come from her." Abraham fell facedown; he laughed
and said to himself, "Will a son be born to a man a hundred
years old? Will Sarah bear a child at the age of ninety?"*

GENESIS 17:15–17 NIV

When Abraham and Sarah heard they were to have a child,
they both laughed. A baby? At their age? How could that be?
Old bodies didn't make babies!

Initially it might have been hard to imagine, but surely when
they thought about how great God is, that He is the Creator
who made everything out of nothing, their laughter stopped.
Considering their own frailty, they could not imagine this
happening. But once they considered God, the tables turned.

Even if during the next nine months they paused to imagine
the impossibility of it all and began to laugh again, the proof
before them—a ninety-year-old woman who showed all the signs
of pregnancy—changed the whole dynamic. If they laughed, it
was *with* God, at this wonderful impossibility that came true.

And God did fulfill the promise flawlessly: "Now the LORD was gracious to Sarah as he had said, and the LORD did for Sarah what he had promised. Sarah became pregnant and bore a son to Abraham in his old age, at the very time God had promised him" (Genesis 21:1–2 NIV).

Oh, the joy Abraham and Sarah must have had following Isaac's safe birth. On a purely human level they delighted in the birth of a child. But when they considered God's promise and the way He brought its fulfillment about, they would have had trouble wrapping their minds around it. How great was their God!

This same God has made us a part of His family. Are we also awestruck at His greatness?

THANK YOU, LORD, FOR THE WONDERFUL
THINGS YOU'VE DONE IN MY LIFE. MAY I NEVER
BECOME BLASÉ TO YOUR POWER.

JEZEBELS IN OUR LIVES

They went back and told Jehu, who said, "This is the word of the LORD that he spoke through his servant Elijah the Tishbite: On the plot of ground at Jezreel dogs will devour Jezebel's flesh. Jezebel's body will be like dung on the ground in the plot at Jezreel, so that no one will be able to say, 'This is Jezebel.'"

2 KINGS 9:36–37 NIV

After assassinating Joram, king of Israel, Jehu headed to Jezreel; he sought the queen mother, Jezebel, who with her husband, Ahab, had led the northern kingdom of Israel into idolatry. The newly anointed King Jehu ordered Jezebel to be thrown down from a tower, where she was trampled by horses.

When Jehu returned to order Jezebel's burial, there was almost nothing left of her. As his men reported back to the new king, they reminded him that this fulfilled Elijah's prophecy (1 Kings 21:23).

Given the opportunity to repent for her sins, Jezebel, unlike her husband, refused. Elijah's prophecy of a gruesome death didn't faze her as it had Ahab. Because the king repented, God did not punish him and kept his nation from harm during his lifetime. Ahab died in battle instead of sharing Jezebel's demise.

Ironically, Jezebel died in Jezreel. This was the hometown

of Naboth, the man she conspired to have murdered because he would not give up his family's land for Ahab to plant a vegetable garden.

Evil may seem to have its day. Though it seems powerful and the "little people" seem helpless, wickedness won't last forever. Our focus should be trusting in God and putting temptations to do evil aside, and God will vindicate us (Psalm 37:1–6). He does not forget us when Satan strikes, nor will the enemy win.

In this harsh, cold world, it may seem that help is far from us. But that is never true. Our Lord never deserts us, and the closer we draw to Him, the more we see Him at work in unexpected places.

The Jezebels in our lives are only temporary. Their power fades in God's own timing.

LORD, WHEN EVIL SEEMS TO BE WINNING,
HELP ME TO KEEP MY EYES ON YOU.

PROTECTED FROM POOR DECISIONS

*When Abram heard that his relative had been taken captive,
he called out the 318 trained men born in his household
and went in pursuit as far as Dan. During the night Abram
divided his men to attack them and he routed them, pursuing
them as far as Hobah, north of Damascus. He recovered
all the goods and brought back his relative Lot and his
possessions, together with the women and the other people.*

GENESIS 14:14–16 NIV

Abram and his nephew Lot prospered in the land God brought them to. Eventually, they had so many sheep—and their shepherds quarreled so much about the grazing—that Abram decided it was time to spread out. So he and Lot agreed to separate. Generous Abram gave Lot the first choice of land, and Lot chose the best-watered property, the plain of the Jordan. But that best grazing was near the pagan city of Sodom.

Sometimes the places we think will be best turn out to be anything but. So it was with Lot's new home. By now Lot was living in Sodom—and he was swept away when the city was attacked and Sodom's defenders ran.

One man who escaped brought Abram news of his nephew's

capture. Though Lot by his selfish choice had brought some of this trouble on himself, Abram hurried to his rescue. This patriarch of Israel, known for his great faith, did what God does for all of us—he stepped in to deliver someone who'd carelessly wandered into trouble.

And God was faithful to Lot, even though he'd settled into a city filled with people who "were wicked and were sinning greatly against the LORD" (Genesis 13:13 NIV). When the Lord later decided to completely destroy Sodom and its wicked sister city, Gomorrah, He made sure that Lot and his family were given the opportunity to escape.

Today, like Lot, even we who follow Jesus can make poor decisions. But our powerful God, who is always in complete control, still protects us. Let's love Him as Romans 8:28 says, and expect Him to work out all things for our good.

LORD, PLEASE KEEP ME FROM FLIRTING WITH SIN. GIVE ME A DESIRE TO HONOR YOU, WHOLLY, EVERY TIME I'M TEMPTED.

GOD'S CONTROL
EVERY DAY

Now the Jordan is at flood stage all during harvest. Yet as soon as the priests who carried the ark reached the Jordan and their feet touched the water's edge, the water from upstream stopped flowing. It piled up in a heap a great distance away, at a town called Adam in the vicinity of Zarethan, while the water flowing down to the Sea of the Arabah (that is, the Dead Sea) was completely cut off. So the people crossed over opposite Jericho.
JOSHUA 3:15–16 NIV

In a mini replay of the Red Sea crossing of the Exodus, all Israel crossed the Jordan River on a dry riverbed.

Though the Red Sea gets most of the attention in Sunday school, this crossing was an important moment in the history of Israel. After they'd wandered for forty years, God was bringing His weary people into the Promised Land. Between them and the land lay a river that had to be passed through by elderly people, pregnant women, and babes in arms. Even going through a small stream would have been challenging for some of them, but this was a river—at flood stage! Stones on the riverbed could have brought them down. A fractious toddler could have ended up face down in the water, having eluded his anxious mother's hand. If anyone pushed or shoved, accidents could have caused much trouble.

Instead of working out lesser logistics for the people to cross safely, God simply erased the dangers. He created a moment of testimony to His greatness by having the ark of the covenant remain midstream while the people walked over a dry riverbed.

God's grace worked in the people's lives at the perfect moment. It works in our lives too. We often think of God's control in our lives in terms of His rescue in dire moments, as He did here at the Jordan. But let's remember that God also controls the less traumatic days of our lives, making good out of all.

Whether we're crossing a trickling stream or a flooding river, let's be sure to acknowledge and thank Him.

LORD, I APPRECIATE YOUR CONTROL
OVER EVERY MOMENT OF MY LIFE.

AN UNRECOGNIZED PLAN

The light from the sun was gone. And suddenly, the curtain in the sanctuary of the Temple was torn down the middle. Then Jesus shouted, "Father, I entrust my spirit into your hands!" And with those words he breathed his last.

LUKE 23:45–46 NLT

In the midst of darkness, Jesus gave up His life. It *was* a dark day for those who had followed Him during His three-year ministry. Where did this leave them? They'd expected Him to bring in a new kingdom on earth. *What kind of kingdom is this?* they must have wondered.

Their Master had given them a few hints of what would happen, but hardly enough for them to have an action plan. They had to move forward in faith because their eyes could see nothing ahead of them.

But the torn temple curtain symbolized the truth that God was no longer separated from His people. Though some leaders in Israel would have preferred a god behind a curtain, one that gave them authority but demanded only legalism in return, God was now giving mankind both the freedom and the responsibilities of a new, spiritual kingdom in Christ. Jesus had brought God the Father to the world through His salvation.

The Spirit was soon to fill Jesus' disciples, and He would show them the plan (John 16:5–14).

Jesus' death completed the act of salvation that God had always had in mind. When Roman soldiers killed Him on the cross, it did not end God's plan. The process advanced through the death of this Lamb of God. No longer would God's people be required to perform regular animal sacrifices, since Jesus had become the onetime substitutionary death for all sin.

For a few days, Jesus' followers must have felt as if God had lost control. But the resurrection soon proved that the seeming tragedy was all just part of His plan.

When our lives seem painful and senseless, trust that God is in control. He may just be working out an unrecognized plan in our lives.

LORD, THANK YOU FOR HAVING PLANS FOR ME THAT I CANNOT SEE. KEEP ME STRONG IN FAITH WHILE YOU BRING THEM TO PASS.

THE SPIRIT'S WORK

Then at evening the same day, being the first day of the week, when the doors were shut where the disciples were assembled, for fear of the Jews, Jesus came and stood in the midst and said to them, "Peace be to you." And when He had said this, He showed them His hands and His side. Then the disciples were glad when they saw the Lord. Then Jesus said to them again, "Peace be to you. As My Father has sent Me, even so I send you." And when He had said this, He breathed on them and said to them, "Receive the Holy Spirit."

JOHN 20:19–22 SKJV

Though Mary Magdalene had run to the disciples with the news that Jesus had risen, they had not seen Him. Some seemed doubtful about her news. So that evening, Jesus appeared to His fearful followers. By showing them His wounds, He proved Himself to them, and when they realized that it truly was Jesus, their hearts rejoiced. None of their fears had been warranted. And the testimony of Mary and the other women *was* true. In preparation for the ministry He was about to place in their hands, Jesus gave them His peace. No longer would they fearfully hide in a room.

As Jesus gave His followers their commission, He also

promised them the Holy Spirit, who would empower them to do God's will and spread the gospel to the nations. Through the Spirit, they would know where to go and what to do for God. Now, when He left them, they need no longer fear.

A few weeks later, at Pentecost, Joel's prophecy that the Spirit would be poured out on all people was fulfilled (Acts 2:16–18). Peter would immediately preach the gospel, fully and freely—and he and the other apostles "turned the world upside down" (Acts 17:6 skjv) with their preaching about Jesus.

The Spirit is still working in lives today—our own lives to share the gospel and the lives of those who need to hear this message. As we allow the Spirit to work in our hearts and minds, we begin to grasp His ultimate control over all things.

LORD, MAY YOUR SPIRIT FILL ME TO DO YOUR WILL
AND GUIDE ME IN THE RIGHT DIRECTION.

A GREAT COMMISSION

And He said to them, "Go into all the world and preach the gospel to every creature. He who believes and is baptized shall be saved, but he who does not believe shall be condemned. And these signs shall follow those who believe: in My name they shall cast out demons; they shall speak with new tongues; they shall take up serpents; and if they drink any deadly thing, it shall not hurt them; they shall lay hands on the sick, and they shall recover." So then, after the Lord had spoken to them, He was received up into heaven, and sat on the right hand of God. And they went out and preached everywhere, the Lord working with them and confirming the word with signs that followed. Amen.

MARK 16:15–20 SKJV

. . . .

The disciples' last in-the-flesh meeting with Jesus occurred when He gave them His detailed orders for ministry. No longer would He physically stand by their side, but He would still work with them and through them. God's protection would be on them, and they would be able to cast out demons and heal the sick.

Perhaps they were a little stunned by this news, but the apostles had no time for questions. Jesus was received into heaven and sat next to God the Father on His throne.

The eleven men obeyed the commission their Master had given them. Not only did their words reach out to people, but God gave them signs that proved their words and mission were true.

Starting this new ministry, in the face of people who hated their message and Master, could not have been easy. But "the Lord [was] working with them." They did not have to come up with the ideas that made ministry successful. God had a plan, and they simply followed it.

May we always do the same—follow the plan that God has for us, the perfect plan that brings honor to Him and benefit to us. He is always in control. Let us take comfort and courage from that fact.

THANK YOU, LORD, FOR GUIDING ME, JUST AS YOU DIRECTED THE APOSTLES' WORK. PLEASE CONTROL ALL I DO FOR YOU AND MAKE IT SUCCESSFUL IN YOUR EYES.

THE TRUSTED KING JAMES VERSION. . . JUST EASIER TO READ

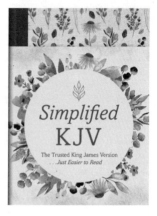

God Is in Control Devotions for Women quotes scripture from the Barbour Simplified KJV. Maintaining the familiarity and trustworthiness of the King James Version, it removes the difficulties of antiquated language and punctuation. Keeping all the original translation work of the 1611 Bible, the Simplified KJV carefully updates old styles that may interfere with your reading pleasure and comprehension today.